Paul & Jeanne Rankin

New Irish Cookery

Paul & Jeanne Rankin

New Irish Cookery

To Hugh, Iris, Richard and Marge

Thanks to our agents Fiona Lindsay and Linda Shanks for their continued support, to Orla Broderick for her help in compiling the recipe lists, to the team at BBC Books, especially Julie Tochel, who had the patience of a saint, to Bren Parkins-Knight at New Crane, and to all the staff at our restaurants and cafés who work so diligently, even when the bosses are away.

Published by BBC Worldwide Limited, Woodlands, 80 Wood Lane, London W12 0TT

First published 2003
© Paul and Jeanne Rankin 2003
The moral right of the authors has been asserted.

Some of the recipes contained in this book are based on recipes that first appeared in *Gourmet Ireland* (BBC Books, 1994) and *Gourmet Ireland 2* (BBC Books, 1995), photographs © Graham Kirk.

New food photography for this edition: Gareth Morgans © BBC Worldwide 2003.

BBC Worldwide would like to thank the following for providing photographs and for granting permission to reproduce copyright material: Alamy 21, 65; Collections 33, 115; Corbis 7, 13, 87, 145, 159; Getty Images 10, 169; Lonely Planet Images 205; New Crane Publishing/Caroline Arber 221, 223.

ISBN 0 563 48878 6

Commissioning Editor: Vivien Bowler
Project Editor: Julie Tochel
Copy-editor: Deborah Savage
Designer: Janet James
Art Director: Linda Blakemore
Art Director for jacket: Pene Parker
Picture Researcher: Miriam Hyman
Production Controller: Kenneth McKay
Food Stylist: Bren Parkins-Knight
Assistant Food Stylist: Rebecca Blackstone
Photography Stylist: Helen Lesur

Printed and bound in Italy by L.E.G.O. spa
Colour separations by Radstock Reproductions Ltd, Midsomer Norton

contents

introduction

Cooking is and has been a very large part of our lives for a very long time. Neither of us had planned to be cooks, yet neither of us can imagine doing anything else for a living. It must just have been meant to be.

Paul grew up in Northern Ireland. His folks were in the clothing business, but lived in a small village on the coast of County Down. His mum, like so many mums, was (and still is) a fine cook. She may have prepared simple fare, but was always committed to quality and first-class produce. Jeanne grew up in Winnipeg, on the prairies in Canada. Of French and northern European extraction, her parents both came from farming backgrounds, but had left the country to pursue academic careers. She grew up in a large family, eating large family meals and, out of necessity, helping out a lot in the kitchen.

Jeanne had always wanted to travel, to get away from those huge expanses of North America and see other lands, other peoples and other cultures. A year of waitressing after high school enabled her to save enough money and she was off to Europe. Paul tried university in Belfast one year, then studied osteopathy in London another before he realized that his heart was elsewhere. He left Britain, headed south, and in Greece he met Jeanne.

To travel takes funds, so Jeanne dragged Paul back to Canada, taught him how to be a waiter, and they both worked hard, usually two jobs at a time. This was really Paul's introduction to the restaurant industry as Northern Ireland would not have been the place to do much dining out in the 1960s and 1970s. He loved the drama of table service, the charm and theatre of being a waiter, and the atmosphere of the great restaurants. Indeed, his passion had been ignited, but he did not yet realize it because he and Jeanne were still dreaming of far-off lands.

From this point on our lives continued together and, after a year and a half, we were set, and off we went to India. A year there had us well in love with Indian food. Just imagine all the foods we encountered. Various regions had their own specialities, techniques and produce. Much of the food was cooked in front of us, on the street. How could we fail to be interested, to be captivated? India led to Australia. A year there working in the restaurant scene opened our eyes in another direction. We were introduced to, and fell in love with, the wine industry. It was while we were there that we became determined to train as chefs and to someday, maybe, even have our own restaurant. But first, more travelling, this time fully aware of the chance to glimpse other cuisines and learn. So we visited Singapore, Malaysia, Thailand, Hong Kong and even spent three months in mainland China (just newly opened to foreigners). Our ongoing love affair with spices and Pan-Asian food in general comes from these years, and has influenced our food dramatically.

Before we could realize our dream and open a restaurant of our own, we needed what we called proper training. Nearly three years back in London, under the watchful eye of Albert Roux, gave us the classical French foundations every chef must acquire. Our knife skills, our cooking techniques, our understanding and respect of food products, and our appreciation of the professional kitchen, all stem from this time. The nature of working in a three-star Michelin restaurant taught us how to work in high-stress situations, to stay cool under pressure, and to be organized. Most of all, we realized that if we could work as hard as we were for someone else, we could certainly do it for ourselves.

We moved back to North America when our first child was on the way. Vancouver gave us a chance to learn Japanese food big time, and also to check out the hotel scene. After a year we headed south to California, once again wanting the opportunity to see wine and food working together. It was here in the Napa Valley that Paul really started to develop his own style as a head chef. Jeanne was his pastry chef. Looking back, we realize that it was the years there that really solidified and brought together all our experiences and knowledge.

And then we returned to Northern Ireland. We bought a bankrupt Indian restaurant and renovated it into a bright airy brasserie. We knew little of the quality and quantity of Irish ingredients, having never cooked there, and were slightly dubious after having been so spoilt for choice in the Napa – but we were blown away, to say the least. The seafood is without a doubt some of the best in the world. Lush pastures guarantee not only fantastic meats, but also incredible dairy products. In those early days there was not a huge variety of locally grown vegetables, but the more traditional ones were exceptional. So we used all these local ingredients and combined them with our knowledge of modern, classic French cooking. Global influences crept in as well and, after a year and a half, our restaurant, Roscoff, was awarded the first Michelin star in the history of Northern Ireland.

It was the media hype that followed that led to our foray into television. When a local TV producer approached us about the possibility of a cookery show, we declared it should be a showcase for Irish foodstuffs, and the country's artisan producers. *Gourmet Ireland* was born. We travelled the length and breadth of the country visiting growers, fishermen and suppliers. We took their products back to a studio kitchen and cooked them in our style, an individual mix of traditional Irish, French and international influences. It seemed to work. Two more series of *Gourmet Ireland* followed, and Paul joined the *Ready Steady Cook* team, and did three series of *The Rankin Challenge*.

The television stuff is fun and exciting, but we have never let go of the restaurant side of things. In fact, 12 years on, we now have a boutique bakery that services three Rankin cafés (and a host of other restaurants, delis and shops) and a family restaurant called Rain City Grill. Roscoff has evolved into the funkier and more casual Cayenne restaurant. Here the menu has become more eclectic in style, with a leaning towards chilli and spice, but the emphasis is still on local ingredients.

At home, with growing children, we realize there is a need for healthy and nutritious food. Luckily, we all enjoy salads and vegetables. We make lots of hearty soups in the winter and serve them with traditional wheaten or soda breads for a filling meal. The whole family loves Chinese and Indian flavours so rice- and noodle-based dishes make frequent appearances throughout the week. We have organic vegetables delivered by a local grower once a week, and also try to buy organic produce from the supermarket. To be honest, Jeanne doesn't find a lot of time to indulge in very much home-baking at the moment, but so it goes.

Hopefully, we are passing on to our kids and customers our passion for cooking with fresh and tasty Irish ingredients. This is so important, not only for our health but also for the survival of true foodstuffs and the grassroots level suppliers. We feel that far too many people get by living off processed foods and accept mass-produced goods that don't really do anyone any favours. In Ireland there is now a fantastic surge in the move towards real foods. Every region has its farmers' markets, organic growers and the like. People are looking for quality. It is a movement in the right direction, one that will preserve not only real cooking traditions but the countryside and waterways as well.

Opposite:
Loin of Venison
with Bacon and
Irish Whiskey Cream
(see page 140)

ireland's larder

Vegetables and Herbs

Some of the best vegetables we have ever tasted have come from this little island. With its temperate climate and all the rain it gets it is a grower's paradise, with perhaps only the wind as the main force to be reckoned with. The polytunnel approach can deal with that, and individual growers up and down the country are doing us proud. Wonderful young carrots, baby bok choy, young beetroot, fennel, parsnips, rocket, leeks are just a few vegetables that we enjoy each year. Way back in the late 1980s, when we were setting up our first restaurant, we had to approach a small grower and ask him to grow items for the restaurant as the north was a wee bit slow to develop. Fortunately, nowadays nearly every corner of Ireland has its own local growers committed to quality, and usually to organic production as well. Consequently, their produce can be found at all sorts of local markets, greengrocers and, very often, can be bought from the farms themselves (watch for signs as you travel the country). It would be impossible even to begin to list these producers here. However, for terrific information about Ireland's small growers and local markets, check out John McKenna's excellent *Bridgestone Shoppers Guide* or, in the north, his *Bridgestone Food Lovers Guide to Northern Ireland* is a must. See also www.bridgestoneguides.com

WILD MUSHROOMS

One of the things we enjoy most in the autumn is getting out to pick wild mushrooms. It is invigorating, healthy and utterly addictive. We often find large quantities of ceps (porcini/penny buns), chanterelles, hedgehogs, saffron milk caps and field mushrooms. However we would never pick a mushroom we were not sure of because there is always a risk that it could be toxic or downright poisonous. We sometimes gather so many that we donate most of them to the restaurant, although we are starting to learn all about drying and pickling them from a knowledgeable Russian friend. It is great fun for the whole family, and has the added bonus of a very delicious and valuable bounty at the end of the day. If you fancy having a go yourself, be sure to either use a good guidebook, or check local colleges or parks for public walks and field trips. The Irish Restaurant Association has guided walks every year, and other organizations must have similar set-ups. We are always asked just where we go, and it must suffice to say, that is our secret. The people of European extraction who have settled here appreciate our local mushrooms though, and, like us, they tend to have their own secret places for searching and picking.

Seafood

FISH

In Ireland you're never more than about an hour's drive away from the sea and, more often than not, you're only about 5–10 minutes away. In addition the island is chock-a-block with rivers and lakes. Is it any wonder it has the best fish we have ever worked with? What seems unusual for such a small island, is that you can get bass, for example, on the west coast, but not on the east. This is because of the Gulf Stream, which flows up the west coast bringing with it exotica like red mullet, John Dory, tuna, crawfish and so on, as well as bass. It's all swings and roundabouts, though, because the east coast gets more prawns and herrings. There is also an abundance of freshwater fish. Salmon, trout, pollan, perch and eel are just a few that spring to mind, but each and every variety is fantastic. The most important factor with any fish is freshness and proper handling. We know you won't be disappointed in any Irish fish if you take time and care when buying it. Most of the fish in our recipes can easily be replaced with other kinds, so think fresh and in season, and try some out.

SHELLFISH

In Ireland we are self-sufficient in all types of shellfish, and in most parts of the country there is usually a small fish shop or friendly supermarket that will try to obtain what you may require. A lot of our shellfish is exported to Spain, France, and England simply because it is so good and people there are willing to pay any price for our top-class products.

The **lobster** in Ireland is, for us, the best in the world. It is recognizable by its blue/black appearance, as opposed to the dark green/brown of the North American variety. The best time to buy it is in high summer, when the weather is good and the fishing is easier. Prices drop to almost half the winter price.

The main **prawns** are the Dublin Bay prawns, sometimes known as scampi or langoustines. They are fished pretty much all over Ireland and are generally available all year round, weather permitting. The Dublin Bay prawn is an absolutely stunning product but it is very fragile as it deteriorates (goes soft and mushy) very rapidly when dead. So, the rule is to buy live ones, or very fresh dead ones, or very nicely cooked ones (difficult to find, though). It's a good idea to buy about 25 per cent more than a recipe calls for as often about a quarter of them may be mushy. Now, before you decide never to bother trying a recipe with Dublin Bay prawns, let us reassure you that they are so good (better than lobster, says Paul) that it is really worth having a go.

It is mostly the large king **scallops** that are available in Ireland, although we do get the queenies – the very small, sweet ones. However, finding any type of scallop in Ireland will depend on the season and where you live. The season runs approximately from November through April almost all over the island.

There are exceptions, though, and these are confusing, so it is better just to trust your fishmonger. It is illegal to dive for scallops in the south, but not in the north. Basically three types of king scallops are available. The best and most difficult to find are diver scallops. Hand-picked from the ocean floor, these are normally the largest, cleanest and most expensive specimens you can possibly buy. They are normally still in the shell, but may be shucked if they are processed by a good supplier. The second type is the dredged scallop. These are fished by boats with dredging nets, which literally scrape the scallops (and everything else) from the ocean bed. This is not an ideal method of fishing as it obviously decimates the environment and also pushes dirt and sand into the shells often making the scallops bruised and gritty. With careful handling however, they can be excellent. The third type is the processed scallop, which may have been either dredged or hand-picked, but the problem with these scallops is that some processors pump them full of water, and thus get a lot more money for less meat. The meat absorbs water easily, up to 50 per cent of its weight, but when you cook the scallops, the water leaks out again, sometimes spoiling the dish and always letting you down in flavour and texture. Most processed scallops have been soaked, but it is very difficult to tell the extent to which this has been done, so it comes down to knowing or trusting the seller.

Our **crabs** can be excellent. There is a lot of the brown variety here, but they can be difficult to buy unless you live near a fishing town or have a reputable fishmonger. Good freshly cooked crab is almost a life-changing experience, so it's worth looking out for them. Although our brown crabs are extremely good, they do not grow as big as, say, the Cornish brown crabs and nor are they as meaty as the American

Dungeness, so it can be hard work to extract whatever flesh is there – but we assure you that it is well worth the effort.

Mussels are available both wild and as farmed rope mussels. Both types are excellent. You can literally pull mussels from the rocks in most parts of the country, although it is a good idea to check the cleanliness of the water / whether it is likely to be affected by industrial waste and other types of pollution with the relevant local authority. Wild mussels are terrific in flavour, but may be more difficult to clean with lots of beard and barnacles to scrape off. Some processors use machines that remove most of this. Another problem with wild mussels is that there sometimes seems to be a pearl in every bite. This has caused us problems in the restaurant at times, because occasionally customers think it means the mussels haven't been cleaned properly. Farmed rope mussels are smaller, have thinner shells and are more expensive. However, the meat is often very plump and sweet, and there is almost always less cleaning involved.

Cockles are widely available, and mostly wild. Cockles are also farmed, but these are often sold by the lorry load to Spain. So, it's either back to the wild where you can dig them up yourself in almost any tidal area, or sourcing from a good supplier.

The **squid** season runs from approximately late September until May when squid are plentiful and cheap. They are also available in the summer months but much more difficult to find. Their size runs from about 15 cm (6 in) to 46 cm (18 in). There are smaller squid around, but they don't seem to be as commercially viable. Large squid often get a bad rap as being chewy and tough. There is a little truth to this, as it is the nature of the beast, but we find that with proper handling they are absolutely excellent. Squid is one of those products that our customers keep coming back for – great value and great flavour.

Lastly, but most famous perhaps, are Ireland's **oysters**. We have some of the very best in the world. Our native oyster has a roundish shell and is often smaller that the Pacific oyster, which is also grown here. The Irish native oyster is shipped to restaurants, hotels and gourmets worldwide. The season is from September to April, so if the month doesn't have an r in it they are out of season. The summer months are the breeding season so the eating season is organized from a conservation point of view.

The Pacific oysters are larger, with long oval shells, and can be very good indeed. They are spawned in warmer waters and transferred to beds around Ireland so they are not subject to the breeding season restrictions of the native oyster. They are available year-round for consumption. However, in those summer months they can be rather fatty, milky and bland. The best time to eat either type is from October to March when they are succulent and firm. If eating raw lean towards the smaller ones, that are no bigger than the span of your hand. The larger ones are good only for cooking in Paul's opinion.

Meat, Game and Poultry

POULTRY

Most poultry nowadays is intensively reared, and you cannot help but wonder what they are fed in order to be ready for slaughter at just 11 weeks old. However, in the last ten years or so a brave few have returned to old-fashioned farming methods, organic or otherwise, and, just as with the vegetable scene, if you look past the supermarkets and take the time to suss out your local scene you will probably find a farmer in your area who produces real chickens, who lay real eggs produced to IOFGA (Irish Organic Farmers & Growers Association) standards. In our opinion, although a proper free range chicken can be more expensive, it has a firmer texture and real flavour, making it well worth the difference in price. Most of this good poultry is found in small pockets across Ireland and is not produced in large enough quantities to be networked across the whole island. Again, a check in the Bridgestone guides (see page 11) will give you great leads no matter which part of Ireland you find yourself in.

PORK

Pork, which has been a firm favourite in the meat department in this country is unfortunately on the decline. Most of it is reared intensively (meaning that the pigs are kept indoors and fed on meal) and in general the public is losing interest and confidence in pork – which is fair enough. The alternative is very-good-indeed rare-breed pork. This comes from older breeds that are more hardy, and more suitable for outside production. They are fed meal pellets of maize, barley and soya with no added antibiotics. (Interestingly enough, this meal is more expensive than meal with antibiotics.) The pigs grow more slowly and have more fat and a lot more flavour. Altogether, this type of pork is a cracking product, but it can be hard to find. Ask your local butcher and, again, check local farmers' markets.

LAMB

Lamb is Paul's favourite meat. No wonder, he grew up on the County Down coast where some of the very best of Irish lamb comes from. The animals there are fed on lush pastures, salted by the sea, and the environment is very small, local and caring. Irish lamb, in general, is 95 per cent grass fed and is only being finished on some grain-based meal before being slaughtered. Most of it nowadays is some sort of Texel or Suffolk cross, which produces a good meaty beastie with a decent-sized eye in the loin. Lamb is, of course, at its best in the spring, when it is also at its most expensive. Later in the year, when the lambs are more mature, they are called hoggets. Many people prefer the stronger flavour of hogget to the mild taste of spring lamb, but this is a matter of personal preference. From Christmas until spring, lamb is probably best avoided if you don't enjoy the stronger flavour.

BEEF

In general, most of the beef in Ireland is of a very high quality. The animals are mostly fed on grass and grain-based meal. Most beef cattle are part Continental cross-breed, such as Limonsin or Belgian Blue, as these have a large girdle structure and little fat. It is hard to find pure Aberdeen Angus or Hereford these days as they are too fatty for most. This is a shame because most people love the meat from these fattier cattle, with more marbling, when they taste it, but shun it when buying beef for themselves and their families because they are trying to think health (less fat, more healthy). This is understandable as no one really wants to eat large slabs of fat, but Paul feels we are heading in the wrong direction. Fatty marbling (the small veins of fat that run through the middle of the muscle) used to be an indication of quality and flavour in meat. This kind of meat is still highly prized in countries like Japan and the US where it is given a Grade A stamp and costs more. The excessive fat covering on fattier animals can be cut off, but there is a very real financial implication for the butcher and the consumer in discarding it. So is there a solution? Paul is not really sure, but it would nice to be given more choice and Paul, for one, wouldn't mind paying more for a really good steak.

GAME

As you can imagine, Ireland has terrific game. Perhaps it doesn't have the tradition to rival the likes of Scotland but, in general, it is still good enough to be called world-class and, indeed, attracts hunters from around the globe. A lot of folk think of game as a rather stinky, quite dodgy form of meat. This impression comes from the days when hunters couldn't eat all the game they had shot and refrigeration was

inadequate or non-existent. So the game was just hung in the cool cellar, sometimes not even gutted, for weeks on end. Of course this treatment produced high, almost inedible, meat. As sometimes happens, the keen punters actually developed a taste for this very mature game, as it was known, and in fact wouldn't touch anything that wasn't well hung. Nowadays, we are a lot more organized and knowledgeable and much game is processed in modern facilities which can be traced back to the hunter. Wild game is even making its way into our supermarkets and speciality butchers, so it's worth keeping an eye out for something seasonal and tasty. A list of wild game available in Ireland would be as follows: venison, pheasant, mallard (wild duck), pigeon, widgeon, grouse, teal, woodcock, snipe, partridge, hare and rabbit. Farmed venison, which is reared on estates throughout Ireland is also an excellent product, fully controlled and organized, but deserves a chapter, or perhaps a book in its own right. Most game is seasonal, which is just as well because it makes it more special and, as in the case of grouse, very reassuring, as it is almost non-existent nowadays. It is worth trying to overcome any prejudices against game as it is normally very high-quality meat which is virtually organic. To find game, keep an eye out at good butchers and supermarkets, especially around Christmas. It's often better to find a butcher or friendly restaurant who will order it in for you. Happy hunting!

Dairy

Dairy produce here in Ireland is fantastic beyond belief. Lush, green pasture means happy, fat cows (and sheep and goats, of course). The best cheese-makers use only the summer milk, when the herds are out to grass. They know that the winter milk, when the animals stay inside and feed on meal and silage is just not quite the same and, as such, might compromise their products. Milk, cream and butter are all superb. And the cheeses well, we have seen Irish cheeses for sale in New York, LA and Vancouver, let alone London and Paris. This in itself speaks volumes. A decade or two ago people would maybe have thought Cheddar and more Cheddar, but the influx of Europeans settling in Ireland has brought artisan skills and a multitude of styles of cheese. We reckon that the St Tola fresh goats' cheese log from Ennis, County Clare easily rivals the best the French can produce. The Coolea from north Cork is as good as any Gouda and the Gabriel, made in the west of County Cork, is better than most Gruyère. The Ardrahan, another cheese from north Cork is simply too luscious to compare to anything – its style and flavour put it in its own league. The list goes on and on.

We found it fascinating to visit various cheese-makers when we were making the *Gourmet Ireland* series. The makers were more than happy to show us their methods and their wares. In fact, if you are touring Ireland, visiting cheese-makers is a great day out. A quick search through the Bridgestone guides offers up suggestions of which ones encourage visitors, and you'll be guaranteed great 'craic' – these artisans tend to be a hospitable lot.

Although many people nowadays shun butter and cream as being fattening and bad for them, we both still firmly believe that a little of anything will not kill you. After all, these are pure and natural products, and must be far easier to digest than margarines full of scary and indigestible oils, and fake dairy products full of chemicals. We know for a fact that butter and cream taste a lot better, and cook a lot better. It's simply a matter of using them in moderation. As you will see in our recipes, we love Irish dairy products and will never give them up.

notes on the recipes

- Eggs are large unless stated otherwise. For baking, eggs should be at room temperature – this helps them to mix more easily with other ingredients.
- Unless otherwise specified use single cream, white wine vinegar, black pepper and vegetable oil for these recipes.
- Wash all fresh produce before preparation.

APPROXIMATE WEIGHT CONVERSIONS

- All of the recipes in this book list both imperial and metric measurements. Conversions are approximate and have been rounded up or down. In a few recipes it has been necessary to modify them very slightly. Follow one set of measurements only; do not mix metric and imperial.
- Cup measurements, which are used by cooks in Australia and America, have not been listed in the recipes here as they vary from ingredient to ingredient. Please use kitchen scales to measure dry/solid ingredients.

SPOON MEASURES

- Spoon measurements are level unless otherwise specified. Cutlery varies so widely that it's worth buying a set of standard spoon measures (from any cook shop).
- 1 teaspoon = 5ml
- 1 tablespoon = 15ml
- 1 Australian tablespoon = 20ml (cooks in Australia should measure 3 teaspoons where 1 tablespoon is specified in a recipe)

CONVERSION TABLES

APPROXIMATE LIQUID CONVERSIONS

metric	imperial	AUS	US
50 ml	2 fl oz	¼ cup	¼ cup
125 ml	4 fl oz	½ cup	½ cup
175 ml	6 fl oz	¾ cup	¾ cup
225 ml	8 fl oz	1 cup	1 cup
300 ml	10 fl oz/½ pint	½ pint	1¼ cups
450 ml	16 fl oz	2 cups	2 cups/1 pint
600 ml	20 fl oz/1 pint	1 pint	2½ cups
1 litre	35 fl oz/1¾ pints	1¾ pints	1 quart

WEIGHTS

25 g	1 oz	400 g	14 oz
50 g	2 oz	425 g	15 oz
85 g	3 oz	450 g	1 lb
100 or 115 g	4 oz	500 g	1 lb 2 oz
140 g	5 oz	550 g	1 lb 4 oz
175 g	6 oz	600 g	1 lb 5 oz
225 g	8 oz	650 g	1 lb 7 oz
250 g	9 oz	700 g	1 lb 9 oz
280 g	10 oz	900 g	2 lb
350 g	12 oz	1.3 kg	3 lb
375 g	13 oz	1.8 kg	4 lb

MEASUREMENTS

5 mm	¼ inch	15 cm	6 inches
1 cm	½ inch	18 cm	7 inches
2.5 cm	1 inch	20 cm	8 inches
5 cm	2 inches	25 cm	10 inches
7.5 cm	3 inches	28 cm	11 inches
10 cm	4 inches	30 cm	12 inches

OVEN TEMPERATURES

Gas	°C	Fan °C	°F	Oven temp.
¼	110	90	225	Very cool
½	120	100	250	Very cool
1	140	120	275	Cool or slow
2	150	130	300	Cool or slow
3	160	140	325	Warm
4	180	160	350	Moderate
5	190	170	375	Moderately hot
6	200	180	400	Fairly hot
7	220	200	425	Hot
8	230	210	450	Very hot
9	240	220	475	Very hot

Ireland has a great tradition of hearty soups and, historically, Irish broth (such as our Chicken, Barley and Parsley Broth on page 30) would be made in Irish households even more often than Irish stew. Paul vividly remembers growing up on large bowls of just such steaming broths. His mum would make a stock from shin of beef before she went to church, then afterwards finish off the broth by adding barley and vegetables. The meat from the shin would be served on the side along with a large bowl of floury potatoes. Now that's a proper meal.

As the various seasons brought a surplus of new and reasonably priced vegetables, the likes of asparagus, tomatoes or leeks would make their way into a soup, but that really was about as exotic as it got in Paul's youth. He does, however, remember craving more of the Smoky Tomato and Bacon Soup (see page 23), but that type of soup was deemed a luxury and so was not for everyday like the broths.

Traditionally, broths and lentil soups are the cornerstones of the Irish soup kitchen. Both use a rich stock, usually made from beef, ham or chicken, although lamb also works extremely well, particularly the shanks.

Soups fit the Irish lifestyle, our climate and our taste buds and they remain extremely popular. Most households in Ireland probably have their own new favourites to stand alongside their family's traditional version of broth. More and more nowadays, our family make and enjoy soups with influences from around the world, from French onion to spicy Mexican bean soup. Seafood chowder is a big favourite at our restaurants; we like to think of it as our own idea, but we really pinched it from the east coast of the United States. And in our cafés we can't take the Onion Soup with Cider and a Cashel Blue Butter (see page 22) off the menu without sparking a small riot amongst our regulars. Jeanne's got the kids hooked on her version of butternut squash soup, which is spiced up with curry and coconut.

Remember, the key to making a soup is to use a good stock and the correct amount of aromatics: onions, carrots, celery, leeks, garlic and the like. People often think of stocks as being quite complex to make, with a bouquet garni and a *mirepoix* of vegetables, but don't be put off. A stock can simply be meat and bones given a long simmering. The addition of aromatics can form the base of the soup itself, and whether or not your soup goes on to be puréed or not is entirely up to you. When you realize how simple soups are, you'll begin to make them more and more. Enjoy!

soups

onion soup with cider and a cashel blue butter

This is a very simple onion soup that can work very well as a base for many variations. What about garnishing it with Cheddar and spring onions, crispy bacon and Gruyère cheese, or even Quattro Formaggi?

Serves 6

2 tablespoons butter

1 kg (2 lb 4 oz) onions, roughly chopped

500 ml (18 fl oz) medium-dry cider

1 tablespoon cider vinegar

A pinch of dried thyme

½ bay leaf

2 litres (3½ pints) chicken stock

225 g (8 oz) potatoes, peeled and diced

Salt and freshly ground pepper

Onion slices, fried in butter, to garnish (optional)

Chopped fresh chervil, to garnish (optional)

FOR THE CASHEL BLUE BUTTER

4 tablespoons butter, softened

2 tablespoons single cream

4 tablespoons Cashel Blue cheese, crumbled

1 tablespoon chopped fresh parsley

1 tablespoon snipped fresh chives

Place a heavy saucepan over a medium heat. Add the butter, then the onions and allow the onions to cook gently for about 15 minutes, or until they are soft and lightly browned. Now add the cider and cider vinegar. Boil until the cider has reduced by about a half. Add the thyme, bay leaf, chicken stock, potatoes and a little salt. Bring to a simmer, then cook for about 15 minutes over a low heat.

Remove the bay leaf and purée the soup in a food processor until smooth. Check the seasoning, adding salt and pepper as necessary.

To make the Cashel Blue butter, have all the ingredients at room temperature. In a bowl, mash or whisk the ingredients together until they are quite well blended.

To serve, ladle the soup into six warm bowls. Add a tablespoon of the Cashel Blue butter to each bowl. Garnish with the fried onion and chervil, if using.

This butter also makes an excellent spread for an hors d'oeuvre and it can be made in larger quantities and stored in the freezer.

smoky tomato and bacon soup

The flavour and the appeal of this soup is much greater than you would expect from such a simple recipe. Paul remembers wanting to devour bowl after bowl of this magical concoction as a child, yet he was never allowed to. With no blender for puréeing, everything had to be pushed through a fine strainer with the back of a spoon, so it was deemed quite a difficult soup and only ever made in fairly small quantities.

Serves 4

2 tablespoons light olive oil

2 onions, finely chopped

250 g (9 oz) piece of smoked bacon, diced

12 large ripe tomatoes, roughly chopped, or two 400 g (14 oz) cans of tomatoes

1 tablespoon tomato purée

Salt and freshly ground black pepper

2 tablespoons chopped fresh parsley, to garnish

6 tablespoons cream, to garnish (optional)

Heat the oil in a large saucepan. Add the onions and bacon and cook for about 5 minutes or until the onions have softened and the bacon is lightly golden, stirring occasionally. Stir in the tomatoes, and the tomato purée. Bring to a simmer, and cook gently for 10–15 minutes until all the flavours are combined. **Process in a** food processor, then pass through a fine strainer. Season to taste. **To serve, ladle** the soup into four warm bowls and garnish with the chopped parsley. Serve at once, garnishing with cream if you wish.

seafood chowder with potato and spring onions

This is a new chowder recipe that we've developed recently, with the addition of tomato and saffron. This influence comes from the San Francisco cioppino, so it's almost like a fish stew. It is very easy, and if you prefer your soups chunky, don't bother to purée it.

Serves 8

25 g (1 oz) butter

1 large onion, weighing about 300 g (10 oz), finely chopped

1 celery stick, finely sliced

85 g (3 oz) button mushrooms, sliced

1 large potato, peeled and cut into 1 cm (½ in) dice

3 tomatoes, cut into 1 cm (½ in) dice

1 tablespoon tomato purée

A pinch of saffron strands (optional)

1 litre (1¾ pints) fish or chicken stock

Salt and freshly ground black pepper

450 g (1 lb) mixed fresh fish fillets, such as hake and salmon, cut into 1 cm (½ in) dice, and large prawns, halved lengthways (if using smaller prawns, leave whole)

125 ml (4 fl oz) whipping cream, to serve (optional)

4 tablespoons finely sliced spring onions, to garnish

Melt the butter in a large saucepan and cook the onion, celery and mushrooms over a medium heat, stirring occasionally, for about 10 minutes until soft.

Add the potato, tomatoes, tomato purée, saffron strands, fish or chicken stock, and a little salt. Bring to the boil, and skim off any scum that rises to the surface. Reduce the heat to a simmer, then cook for 15 minutes until the vegetables are soft.

Purée half the mixture in a food processor, then return it to the pan. Taste and adjust the seasoning. Bring back to the boil and add the fish. Stir in most of the cream, if using, saving just a few spoonfuls for the garnish. When the chowder has returned to the boil, remove from the heat and leave to stand for 5 minutes.

Ladle into eight warm soup bowls and drizzle the remaining cream over the soup. Garnish with the spring onions, and serve immediately.

mussels with potato and garlic

This is a bit of a beach-barbecue type of recipe, a simple, earthy one-pot dish that almost anyone could cook. It is tasty with a good splash of cream – and without it too.

Serves 4

1.5 kg (3 lb 5 oz) live mussels
50 ml (2 fl oz) dry white wine
1 fresh thyme sprig
1 fresh parsley sprig
3 garlic cloves, sliced
100 g (4 oz) leeks, thinly sliced
400 g (14 oz) potatoes, peeled and cut into 1 cm (½ in) dice
1 tablespoon chopped fresh parsley
Salt and freshly ground black pepper

Wash the mussels in plenty of cold water, pulling away the hairy beards as you go. Discard any that are not closed, or do not close if tapped with a knife.

Bring 200 ml (7 fl oz) of water and the white wine to the boil in a large saucepan. Add the herb sprigs and garlic and simmer for 1 minute. Add the mussels, bring to a vigorous boil, and cook for 45 minutes until they have all opened. Discard any that do not open. Immediately drain in a colander, catching all the juices in a bowl.

Strain the juices into a clean saucepan and add the leeks and potatoes. Cook over a moderate heat for about 7 minutes or until the potatoes are tender.

While the potatoes are cooking, pull the mussels from their shells. Leave a few in their shells to garnish.

To serve, add the mussels and chopped parsley to the potato and leek broth, and warm thoroughly. Check and adjust the seasoning to taste. Serve in four warm bowls, garnished with the mussels left in their shells.

celeriac soup with saffron and scallops

We learned to cook and love this simple soup while working at Le Gavroche, Albert Roux's three-star Michelin restaurant in London. So it's not Irish at all, but very French. It's even better, of course, made with wonderful Irish produce, and could be considered to be a poor man's version of chowder.

Serves 4

25 g (1 oz) butter

1 medium onion, sliced

½ bulb celeriac, peeled and cut into 2 cm (¾ in) dice

A pinch of saffron strands

1 bay leaf

1 litre (1¾ pints) water or fish or chicken stock

Salt and freshly ground white pepper

4 large scallops, without corals, finely sliced

8 tablespoons whipping cream, to garnish (optional)

1 tablespoon chopped fresh parsley, to garnish

Melt the butter in a large saucepan over a medium heat. Add the onion and sauté for about 10 minutes, until it is just starting to colour. Add the celeriac, saffron strands, bay leaf, water or stock and salt. Bring to the boil. Reduce the heat, and simmer gently for about 30 minutes.

Remove from the heat. Purée the soup in a food processor to a nice smooth consistency, and adjust the seasoning as necessary.

Season the scallop slices with a little salt and pepper, and place a few of them in the bottom of warm bowls. Ladle the soup on top. The heat of the soup will cook the scallop pieces just perfectly.

Garnish with a swirl of the cream, if using, and a sprinkle of parsley. Serve at once.

red lentil and ham soup

To us, red lentil soup is infinitely better when made with a good meat stock. Shank is the favourite because of its rich textures and the flavour it gives. Try making this soup with lamb shanks, and then adding a little garlic, chilli and lemon juice for a Middle-Eastern version… and we don't mean County Wexford.

Serves 8

1 ham shank, weighing about 900 g (2 lb), or 500 g (1 lb 2 oz) piece of ham or bacon, or a ham bone

1 large onion, finely chopped

1 celery stick, finely diced

1 medium carrot, grated

1 large potato, peeled and cut into 1 cm (½ in) dice

200 g (8 oz) red lentils, washed and drained

Salt and freshly ground pepper

Chopped fresh parsley, to garnish

Place the meat in a large saucepan with about 3.5 litres (6 pints) of cold water. Bring to the boil and skim off any scum that rises to the surface. Simmer the ham shanks (or ham bone, if using) for 2–3 hours or until the meat is very tender (this will not take as long if you are using a piece of ham or bacon).

Forty-five minutes before the end of the cooking time, add the vegetables and the lentils. Skim the soup as it comes back to the boil. The soup is ready when the lentils are cooked, but it will taste much better if it is left to stand for 4–5 hours or overnight and then reheated. Season to taste.

To serve, remove the ham bone, or if using a piece of ham or bacon either save it for another use or chop or flake the meat into small pieces and return to the soup. Ladle into eight warm soup bowls and sprinkle with the parsley. You can remove and serve the potatoes on the side, if you wish.

chicken, barley and parsley broth

Paul grew up with this soup and it is a firm favourite in our household to this day. Try substituting shin of beef for the chicken, add a few leeks and you've got a real Irish broth.

Serves 6–8

2.25 kg (5 lb) boiling chicken
400 g (14 oz) onions, chopped
250 g (9 oz) barley, soaked overnight
200 g (8 oz) carrots, grated (optional)
2 tablespoons salt
1 tablespoon freshly ground white pepper
50 g (2 oz) fresh parsley, finely chopped

Wash and clean the chicken and place in a large saucepan with 3.9 litres (7 pints) of cold water. Bring to the boil over a medium heat and skim off any scum that rises to the surface. Add another 300 ml (½ pint) of cold water (this addition helps to release the scum) and simmer gently for about 5 hours, skimming occasionally.

Remove the chicken and allow to cool. Add the onions, soaked barley and carrots (if using) to the broth and simmer for about 30 minutes.

When the chicken is cool enough to handle, remove the meat from the carcass, discarding the skin. Chop it into bite-size pieces and return to the broth. Season with salt and pepper. Just before serving the broth, add the parsley.

spiced carrot soup with basil

I don't know about you, but we are fed up with the ubiquitous carrot and coriander soup.
Try this one and you may never go back.

Serves 4

50 g (2 oz) butter

2 onions, chopped

2 tablespoons chopped root ginger

2 teaspoons coriander seeds, crushed or ground

2 teaspoons curry powder

Salt and freshly ground black pepper

450 g (1 lb) carrots, chopped

1 litre (1³/₄ pints) chicken or vegetable stock

1–2 teaspoons sugar

1 teaspoon finely grated orange zest

150 ml (¹/₄ pint) orange juice

2 tablespoons roughly chopped basil leaves

4 tablespoons cream, to garnish (optional)

2 tablespoons pine nuts, toasted, to garnish

Melt the butter in a large saucepan over a medium heat and add the onions. Sauté for about 10 minutes, until soft and translucent. Add the ginger, coriander seeds, curry powder, salt and carrots, and continue to cook for another 10 minutes, stirring occasionally to prevent the mixture catching on the bottom of the saucepan.

Add the stock and simmer for 20 minutes, or until the carrots are completely tender. Remove from the heat and purée in a food processor.

Taste the soup for seasoning, and adjust as needed. Add the sugar, orange zest and orange juice, bring back to a simmer, then stir in the basil and ladle into warm soup bowls. Top with a spoonful of the cream if using, and the toasted pine nuts. Serve at once.

From a chef's point of view, starters are one of the most exciting things to make. You can be whimsical and you can have fun, and you don't feel that you have to balance things to make a meat and two veg plate. You can be daring and you can be creative but, perhaps most importantly, you can keep things straightforward and pure if the product suggests so. Would anyone not be delighted with Grilled Dublin Bay Prawns with Garlic Butter (see page 43), or a fresh Old-Fashioned Salmon Mayonnaise (see page 38) served with melba toast? Our favourite starters are so simple, so pure, and so very, very tasty.

In restaurants nowadays it has become fashionable to order two starters instead of a starter and a main course. Jeanne (and a lot of other women) much prefer to eat like this. Actually, Jeanne has done this for years and admits that it has the added bonus of leaving room for a decadent pudding.

More often than not a good starter can be converted (or extended) into a light lunch dish by just making each portion a little larger and serving something on the side. For example, our Creamy Leek and Prawn Tart (see page 54) makes a wonderful uncomplicated starter. All the hard work has been done ahead of time, so it is simply a case of slice and serve. But by simply making the portion a little larger, adding a green salad and maybe some roast peppers, it can become a cracking lunch dish.

A word of caution for when you are having a dinner party or entertaining friends. Choose a dish that you will find undemanding and that's easy to serve and present. There is nothing more stressful, and therefore guaranteed to ruin your mood or appetite, than taking on a dish that is too adventurous or too complicated, and then having a disaster. And it doesn't just happen to you, it has happened to everyone, including us – honestly. Which is why nowadays we just serve soup at our dinner parties… only joking!

starters and light dishes

baked goats' cheese with roast beetroot

Some marriages seem made in heaven and this one certainly is. Each flavour is strong enough to balance the other, yet remains distinct. The dish has nice texture contrasts too.

Serves 4

450 g (1 lb) baby beetroot

450 g (1 lb) goats' cheese

1 tablespoon walnut oil

60 g (2½ oz) coarse home-made breadcrumbs

Mixed salad leaves, to serve

60 g (2½ oz) walnuts, roasted and skinned, to garnish

FOR THE WALNUT VINAIGRETTE

1 teaspoon Dijon mustard

Salt and freshly ground black pepper

2 teaspoons white wine vinegar

50 ml (2 fl oz) peanut oil

50 ml (2 fl oz) walnut oil

First make the walnut vinaigrette. Dissolve the mustard and a dash of salt and pepper in the vinegar. Whisk or stir in the oils. Taste for seasoning and adjust, if necessary. Reserve.

To prepare the beetroot, preheat the oven to 160°C/325°F/Gas 3. Wash and trim each bulb of beetroot, then wrap the bulbs in some foil and bake for about an hour.

Remove from the oven and allow to cool. Peel carefully. Slice into 5 mm (¼ in) thick rounds and marinate these slices in some of the vinaigrette.

To prepare the goats' cheese, turn up the oven to 190°C/375°F/Gas 5. Peel the cheese of any rind and slice into 2 cm (¾ in) thick rounds. Brush with the walnut oil and coat evenly with the breadcrumbs.

Bake for about 10 minutes; the cheese will be heated through and melting at the edges.

To serve, dress the salad leaves with the vinaigrette and place in the centre of each plate. Place the goats' cheese on top. Arrange several slices of beetroot around the salad and drizzle with a bit more of the vinaigrette. Garnish with the roasted walnuts, sprinkling them around and over the salad and beetroot.

smoked haddock tartlets with watercress and mustard hollandaise

Why do smoked fish and egg complement each other so well? We aren't sure why, but they definitely do. If you don't want to use smoked haddock, any smoked fish will do, and if you don't fancy making Hollandaise, topping each tartlet with a poached egg and a little melted butter works too.

Serves 4

750 g (1 lb 10 oz) naturally smoked haddock fillets

600 ml (1 pint) milk

Salt

1 bunch of watercress

Butter

4 cooked 10–12 cm (4–4½ in) tartlet cases, made with Savoury Shortcrust Pastry (see page 234); Puff Pastry (see pages 233–4) also works well

FOR THE MUSTARD HOLLANDAISE

3 egg yolks

250 g (9 oz) unsalted butter, chilled and diced

1 tablespoon Dijon mustard

1 teaspoon lemon juice

Salt and freshly ground white pepper

Preheat the oven to 200°C/400°F/Gas 6.

First make the mustard Hollandaise. Place the egg yolks and a teaspoon of cold water in a ceramic or stainless steel saucepan and place over a pan half-full of simmering water. Whisk until the egg yolks are smooth and thick.

Whisk in the cold, diced butter, a cube at a time, until all the butter has been absorbed and the sauce looks thick and creamy. Season with the mustard, lemon juice and salt and pepper. Keep in a warm, but not too hot, place.

Trim the haddock fillets, removing all the bones carefully.

Pour the milk into a wide saucepan and bring to a simmer. The milk needs to be seasoned with salt but the amount required depends on how salty the haddock is, which really does vary depending on the source of the product. Poach the haddock in the milk, lightly covered with greaseproof paper, for 3–4 minutes. Allow the haddock to cool in the milk.

When cool enough to handle, peel off the skin and break the haddock flesh into large flakes onto a microwave-safe dish. Set aside.

Pick through the watercress, removing the stems and any yellow leaves. Wash and then drop into boiling, salted water. Strain immediately and cool quickly under cold water. Squeeze gently till the watercress is almost dry and place it on the dish alongside the smoked haddock. Dot the watercress with butter and then cover with clingfilm.

To serve, reheat the fish and watercress in the microwave (1 minute on full power) and warm the tartlet cases in the oven. Spoon the watercress evenly into the tartlet cases and top with the smoked haddock, then a generous dollop of Hollandaise. Serve immediately.

old-fashioned salmon mayonnaise

Salmon mayonnaise has been served in Irish country houses and restaurants for generations. Although it keeps well in the fridge, we feel it is at its very best if it has never seen a fridge and is served freshly made at room temperature, with melba toast.

Serves 4

FOR THE POACHING LIQUID
150 ml (¼ pint) dry white wine
1 tablespoon vinegar
300 ml (½ pint) water
6 peppercorns
1 fresh parsley sprig with stalk
2 teaspoons salt

FOR THE SALMON MAYONNAISE
450 g (1 lb) fresh salmon fillet, skinned
5 tablespoons mayonnaise
2 teaspoons Dijon mustard
½ tablespoon finely chopped gherkins
½ tablespoon chopped capers
1½ teaspoons chopped fresh dill
1½ teaspoons snipped fresh chives
Mixed salad leaves, to garnish
A few fresh dill sprigs, to garnish

Combine the ingredients for the poaching liquid in a small saucepan and bring to the boil.

Meanwhile check the salmon for bones. Cut off any brown flesh and cut the remaining flesh into 6–8 cubes. Add the salmon to the poaching liquid and simmer for 3 minutes. Remove the saucepan from the heat and allow to cool.

Transfer the salmon to a medium-sized bowl. Flake the flesh, keeping the flakes large and generously sized. Fold in the mayonnaise, mustard, gherkins, capers and herbs, garnish with the salad leaves and dill, and serve at room temperature.

smoked mackerel pâté with fresh herbs

The success of this recipe, like so many others, depends upon obtaining first-class ingredients. Perhaps more than any other fish, mackerel needs to be sparklingly fresh to get the best out of it. So, shop around to find the best smoked mackerel you can.

Serves 6–8

500 g (1 lb 2 oz) smoked mackerel fillets
140 g (5 oz) unsalted butter, softened
1 tablespoon Dijon mustard
2–3 tablespoons lemon juice
Salt and freshly ground black pepper
A good pinch of cayenne pepper
2 tablespoons capers, rinsed well and roughly chopped
2 tablespoons snipped fresh chives
2 tablespoons roughly chopped fresh dill
Mixed salad leaves, to garnish

Pull the skin off each mackerel fillet, scrape away the very dark flesh underneath the skin and discard it. You don't need to be too fussy over this. We do it simply because the dark flesh can look unpleasant sometimes, and occasionally it has a strong fishy taste. Run your fingers over the fillets to check for bones, and remove any you find.

Roughly chop the mackerel fillets and divide into two equal piles. Purée one pile in a food processor with the butter, mustard, lemon juice, a little salt and pepper and the cayenne pepper. Taste for seasoning and adjust. Scrape this mackerel butter into a clean bowl and mix in the capers and herbs and the second pile of chopped mackerel. The pâté is now finished and can be spooned into ramekins or a pâté dish.

Alternatively, we like to form it into a roll with clingfilm or foil. To do this, simply spread the clingfilm or foil on a flat surface and spoon the pâté onto one end to form a large sausage shape. Roll the pâté in the clingfilm or foil to make a neat cylinder and twist the ends to seal it tightly.

Chill the pâté for at least 2 hours before serving. Cut into small slices and garnish with the salad leaves.

crabcakes with a lemon-garlic mayonnaise

These are very meaty, luxurious crabcakes bound with a little minced fish, and they are just wonderful! It may seem to be stating the very obvious, but do remember that the quality of the crabmeat is the most important factor here. Good-quality fresh or frozen crabmeat works well, but canned is absolutely unacceptable.

Serves 4–6

2 tablespoons butter
2 tablespoons diced red pepper
4 tablespoons finely sliced spring onion
2 tablespoons finely chopped celery
200 g (8 oz) fresh hake or whiting, boned and skinned, or scallops, without corals
450 g (1 lb) fresh or frozen crabmeat
1 egg
1 tablespoon chopped fresh parsley
1 tablespoon chopped fresh basil
1 tablespoon Dijon mustard
200 g (8 oz) fresh breadcrumbs (1/8 of a loaf)
Salt and freshly ground pepper
1 tablespoon vegetable oil

FOR THE LEMON-GARLIC MAYONNAISE
2 egg yolks
2 garlic cloves, finely sliced
1–2 tablespoons lemon juice, to taste
Grated zest of 1 lemon
1/4 teaspoon salt, or to taste
125 ml (4 fl oz) light olive oil
125 ml (4 fl oz) vegetable oil

Melt 1 tablespoon of the butter in a small saucepan and sweat the pepper, spring onions and celery until soft, about 5 minutes. Allow to cool and then place in a bowl.

Process the fresh fish in a food processor to make a rough purée. Add the crabmeat, egg, herbs, mustard and 100 g (4 oz) of the breadcrumbs. Taste for seasoning and add a little salt and pepper if necessary.

Roll the crabmeat mixture into balls just a little larger than a golf ball and dip in the remaining 100 g (4 oz) breadcrumbs. Finally form the balls into little cakes by pressing them down lightly.

To make the lemon garlic mayonnaise, combine the egg yolks, garlic, 1 tablespoon of the lemon juice, the lemon zest and the salt in a food processor. Blend for a few seconds and then slowly add the oils in a steady stream until emulsified. Taste and adjust the amount of lemon juice and salt if needed. Set aside.

Melt 1 tablespoon of the butter in a large frying pan with the vegetable oil. Sauté the crabcakes over a moderate heat until nicely golden and heated right through. This will take about 3–4 minutes on each side. Drain on kitchen paper and serve with the lemon-garlic mayonnaise.

asparagus and wild mushroom bruschetta

It is amazing how certain dishes have become world-famous over the past few decades – quiches, pizzas, spaghetti, hamburgers, to name just a few. Bruschetta is another, and nowadays you are as likely to find it on the menu in West Cork as in New York, Dubai, Sydney or Florence. Each bruschetta would be different, of course, but each would be a slice of toasted or grilled bread topped with something tasty. What could be simpler?

Serves 4

FOR THE MUSHROOM *DUXELLE*

125 g (4½ oz) chopped onions

3 garlic cloves, crushed

50 g (2 oz) dried porcini mushrooms, soaked then drained

450 g (1 lb) button mushrooms, roughly chopped

4 tablespoons extra-virgin olive oil, mixed with 2 teaspoons of truffle oil (optional)

Salt and freshly ground black pepper

FOR THE BRUSCHETTA

4 slices of country bread or baguette

Olive oil

1 garlic clove (optional)

FOR THE ASPARAGUS

450 g (1 lb) asparagus spears

Salt

TO GARNISH

A few sautéed mushrooms

A few salad leaves

Fresh parsley or chervil sprigs

To make the mushroom *duxelle*, fry the onions and garlic in 2 tablespoons of the olive oil in a large saucepan. When they are soft and transparent, add the porcini and button mushrooms and cook for about 10 minutes. Allow the mixture to cool a little before processing in a food processor until coarsely chopped. There should be texture and shape left in the mushrooms. Season generously with salt and pepper and a little of the olive oil and truffle oil mixture (if using).

To make the bruschetta, preheat the grill. Brush each side of the country bread or baguette slices with a little olive oil. If you like garlic, rub each slice with a peeled clove as well. Toast under the preheated grill until crisp.

Break off any very tough parts of the asparagus and, if the skin is tough, peel the spears carefully. Cook in boiling, salted water for 4–8 minutes, depending on the size. Drain them carefully and set aside.

To serve, spread the hot mushroom *duxelle* generously on the toasted slices and set in the centre of warm plates. Top with the asparagus spears and drizzle with the remaining olive oil and truffle oil mixture. Garnish with the sautéed mushrooms, salad leaves and sprigs of parsley or chervil.

grilled dublin bay prawns with garlic butter

Freshness is the most important factor when buying prawns, so always buy seafood from a reliable source. Luckily in Ireland we are blessed with plenty of fresh live prawns. Years ago, we might not have been happy to put our names to such a simple dish as this but, as we've matured and learned more, we have realized that simplicity is often best.

Serves 4

12 large, very fresh, raw Dublin Bay prawns (also known as langoustines or scampi), heads still on
Salt and freshly ground pepper

FOR THE GARLIC BUTTER
200 ml (7 fl oz) dry white wine
2 shallots, finely chopped
125 g (4½ oz) unsalted butter, softened
½–1 tablespoon finely chopped garlic
2 tablespoons chopped fresh parsley
1 tablespoon chopped fresh tarragon
2 tablespoons Pernod (optional)
Salt and freshly ground white pepper
A squeeze of lemon juice (optional)

First make the garlic butter. In a small saucepan boil the wine with the shallots until reduced by half. Now blend the butter, herbs and Pernod, if using, with the white wine and shallot reduction in a food processor until well mixed. The amount of garlic depends on how much you like garlic. Taste the garlic butter carefully for salt and pepper, and add some lemon juice if you feel it needs it.

Preheat the grill to high.

Working on a large cutting board with a large chef's knife, split the prawns lengthways from head to tail and remove any of the dark intestinal tract from the tail. Crack each claw by tapping it with the back of your knife.

Arrange the prawns close together in the grill tray, open sides facing upwards. Season lightly with salt and pepper and spread the garlic butter very generously over the prawns. Cook the prawns for 5 minutes on the lowest rack of the grill. Shake the tray occasionally, to prevent the butter from burning and to mix in those wonderful juices.

Serve immediately, with lots of bread for sopping up the tasty garlic butter. Paul finds the best part of this dish is sucking the shells and claws to savour every last drop of flavour.

smoked salmon and wheaten bread millefeuilles, with marinated red onion

Smoked salmon and wheaten bread are consumed in vast quantities all over Ireland. This is our version, which is really just a fancy, double-decker sandwich. It's great though! A coarse, stoneground wholemeal is the best bread to use.

Serves 4

FOR THE MARINATED ONION

1 red onion, very finely chopped

1 tablespoon rice wine vinegar

1 tablespoon sugar

FOR THE MILLEFEUILLES

200 g (8 oz) Wheaten Bread (see page 226)

300 g (10 oz) smoked salmon

50 g (2 oz) cream cheese

2 tablespoons crème fraîche

1 small bunch of fresh chives, finely snipped

FOR THE DRESSING

3 tablespoons double cream

Juice of ¼ lemon

Salt

TO SERVE

1 bunch of mustard cress

½ cucumber, peeled, seeded and thinly sliced

4 radishes, thinly sliced

Mixed salad leaves

1½ tablespoons extra-virgin olive oil

Marinate the finely chopped red onion in the rice wine vinegar and sugar for 5–10 minutes.

For the millefeuilles slice the wheaten bread into twelve 10 x 10 cm (4 x 4 in) squares each 5 mm (¼ in) thick. Slice the smoked salmon into eight even slices.

Mix together the cream cheese and the crème fraîche. Spread each slice of wheaten bread with the cheese mixture. Lay the slices of smoked salmon on top of eight of the wheaten bread slices. Sprinkle the eight slices with the marinated red onion.

Start to build four millefeuille by placing four slices of topped bread on top of four others. Top each one with one of the remaining four slices of wheaten bread and finish with a generous sprinkling of the chives.

To make the dressing, mix the cream with the lemon juice and salt to taste.

Place a millefeuille in the centre of each plate and arrange around it the mustard cress, cucumber, radishes and salad leaves. Drizzle with the dressing and the olive oil.

warm potato and goats' cheese flans

A real winner for vegetarians, this is one of Jeanne's favourite dishes. We feel that the potato and goats' cheese go so very well together here: the potato cuts into the richness of the cheese and the cream to produce a silky, yet rustic texture.

Serves 4

200 g (8 oz) potatoes, peeled and roughly cut into chunks
125 ml (4 fl oz) milk
125 ml (4 fl oz) whipping cream
Salt and freshly ground pepper
140 g (5 oz) firm goats' cheese, crumbled
3 egg yolks
1 tablespoon butter, softened, for greasing

TO SERVE

1 small bunch of rocket leaves, finely sliced
8 anchovies, soaked in milk for ½ hour
12 black olives, stoned and roughly chopped
1–2 tablespoons good-quality capers, drained and rinsed
4 tablespoons extra-virgin olive oil
Grilled focaccia or crusty bread, to serve (optional)

Preheat the oven to 160ºC/325ºF/Gas 3.

Cook the potatoes in salted, boiling water until just tender. Drain and return to the saucepan with the milk and cream. Simmer for 4–5 minutes, until the liquid thickens slightly.

Remove from the heat and purée in a food processor or, if you prefer a more rustic texture simply mash roughly with a potato masher. Season with salt and pepper and allow to cool for a few minutes before stirring in the goats' cheese and egg yolks.

Generously grease four 150 ml (¼ pint) ramekins or ovenproof cups with the butter. Pour the potato and goats' cheese mixture into them and cover with foil.

Place an ovenproof dish in the oven and pour in some boiling water to make a bain-marie. Place the ramekins or cups in the bain-marie and bake for 4–5 minutes, or until just set.

Remove from the oven and allow to cool for 15–20 minutes before serving. Alternatively, you can cook them well in advance and simply reheat them in the bain-marie just before serving.

To serve, divide the sliced rocket leaves, anchovies, olives, capers and oil between four plates. Carefully turn out the flans in the centre of each plate and serve with grilled focaccia or crusty bread, if you wish.

potato ravioli with black truffle, garlic and anchovy

We wondered if we should include this recipe, because the potato is virtually the only 'Irish' thing about it. However, the recipe was conceived in Ireland, by an Irishman, in our restaurant in Ireland, so we decided that is Irish enough for us.

Serves 4

FOR THE FILLING

8 tablespoons butter

1 small onion, finely chopped

3 garlic cloves, finely chopped

450 g (1 lb) potatoes, peeled and cut into 1 cm (½ in) dice

175 ml (6 fl oz) milk

1 small black truffle, finely chopped

3 tablespoons finely chopped fresh parsley

Salt and freshly ground black pepper

6 anchovy fillets

Fresh flatleaf parsley leaves, to garnish

FOR THE RAVIOLI

280 g (10 oz) plain strong flour ('00' type is the best)

½ teaspoon salt

2 large eggs, beaten

1 tablespoon vegetable or light olive oil

1 egg, beaten, for sealing the edges

Flour, for dusting

First make the filling. Heat 2 tablespoons of the butter in a large frying pan. Add the onion and a third of the chopped garlic and sauté for about 3 minutes. Add the potatoes and milk and cover tightly. Cook over a low heat until very tender, making sure the potatoes don't stick to the pan.

Mash the potatoes with 2 tablespoons of the butter, half the truffle and 2 tablespoons of the chopped parsley. Season and set aside.

To make the pasta dough, place the flour and salt in a large bowl and make a well in the centre. Add the eggs and vegetable or olive oil and, with your hands, mix it together to make a soft and pliable dough. Add a little water if necessary. Turn the dough out onto a floured work surface and knead until smooth and shiny.

Use a pasta machine to do the final kneading. Pass the pasta through the rollers on their widest setting and fold it over on itself. Repeat this about a dozen times. This will really bring the dough together. If you make more than you need the dough can be stored, wrapped tightly in clingfilm, for several days in the fridge or for 1 month in the freezer.

To prepare the ravioli, use a pasta machine to roll the pasta to the width of the machine and to about 30 cm (12 in) long. Cut the dough into thin strips. On one side of each of the strips, place small mounds of potato mixture at 7.5 cm (3 in) intervals. Brush the edges of the strips and between the potato mounds with the beaten egg, then fold the other half over the potato mounds. Seal by pressing along the edges and between the mounds around the stuffing. Using a pastry wheel or knife, cut the ravioli into 6 cm (2½ in) squares and place on a tray dusted lightly with flour.

When ready to cook, dust off any excess flour carefully, and cook in boiling, salted water until the ravioli rise to the surface, about 2–3 minutes. Drain well and arrange on warm plates.

In a small saucepan, melt the rest of the butter and then add the anchovies, the remaining truffle, chopped parsley and garlic, and a little pepper. Taste for seasoning and spoon the mixture over the ravioli. Garnish with the flatleaf parsley leaves and serve immediately.

carpaccio of beef with roast aubergines and balsamic vinegar

Classically, carpaccio was eaten without any garnish, and just a little spicy mayonnaise. We find it much more interesting to serve it with these roast aubergines. We like their softness, which complements the softness of the raw beef. We also enjoy eating carpaccio with almost any other vegetable or salad garnish, especially with mushrooms or artichokes.

Serves 4

2 small aubergines
8 garlic cloves
8 tablespoons light olive oil, plus extra for serving
280 g (10 oz) beef fillet

TO SERVE
2 tablespoons coarse sea salt
1 teaspoon cracked black peppercorns
8 tablespoons balsamic vinegar
Mixed salad leaves
Parmesan cheese shavings
Crusty country bread

Cut each aubergine into four thick slices and gently crush the garlic cloves in their skins. Heat the oil in a heavy frying pan and fry the aubergine slices for 5 minutes on each side together with the garlic. Allow to cool.

Thinly slice the beef fillet into eight pieces. Gently pound the slices between two pieces of oiled clingfilm, until very thin. Try to ensure an even thickness, that is, that one side of a slice is not any thicker than the other side. Arrange these slices carefully on four plates.

To serve, sprinkle the beef with the sea salt and peppercorns. Drizzle the beef slices with the vinegar. Carefully arrange the aubergine slices, garlic and some salad leaves attractively on each plate. Sprinkle the Parmesan shavings over all of these and top with a little oil. Serve with crusty country bread.

spicy leek and goats' cheese soufflés

Soufflés are downright fun and much easier than most people think. If you are careful at every stage, perfect results should follow every time. If not, well, think of it as a funky omelette and better luck next time.

Serves 6

50 g (2 oz) butter, plus extra for greasing

140 g (5 oz) leeks, washed, trimmed and finely sliced

50 g (2 oz) plain white flour

250 ml (9 fl oz) milk

50 g (2 oz) sun-dried tomato, finely sliced

A pinch of white pepper

A pinch of cayenne pepper

A pinch of grated nutmeg

1 small green chilli, finely chopped (optional)

1 teaspoon salt

3 egg yolks

140 g (5 oz) goats' cheese, grated or finely crumbled

8 egg whites

Preheat the oven to 190°C/375°F/Gas 5 and generously grease six little ramekins or ovenproof cups, about 6–10 cm (2–4 in) in diameter.

Melt the 50 g (2 oz) of butter in a saucepan and, when it starts to foam, add the leeks and cook slowly for about 3 minutes, until they start to soften. Add the flour to the saucepan and mix well. Slowly add the milk, stirring continuously, and continue to stir over a medium heat until the sauce has thickened. This will take about 5–10 minutes.

Remove the saucepan from the heat and add the sun-dried tomato, the pepper, cayenne, nutmeg, chilli (if using), ½ teaspoon of the salt and the egg yolks. Stir to combine and then, lastly, add the cheese, reserving 1–2 tablespoons for the tops of the soufflés.

Whisk the egg whites with the remaining salt until stiff. Add about one-third to the yolk mixture and stir together until smooth. Finally, gently fold in the remaining two-thirds of the whites being careful not to overmix.

Spoon the mixture into the ramekins or cups, and sprinkle the remaining cheese on top (at this point you can keep the soufflés in the fridge for about one hour if you like).

Place the soufflés in a bain-marie and bake for 15 minutes. They should be well risen and be golden crusty brown on top. Serve immediately.

warm goats' cheese with grilled vegetables

Warm goats' cheese is one of life's simple pleasures. It seems to lend itself to any vegetable dish, making a superb first course or a perfect light lunch. The vegetables can be grilled on a barbecue or under a grill, and can be prepared ahead of time and kept in the olive oil, with freshly chopped herbs such as basil, thyme and parsley. A little pile of salad leaves under the grilled cheese makes it a more substantial meal.

Serves 4–6

Half a large, fresh goats' cheese log, approximately 550 g (1 lb 4 oz)

2 tablespoons softened butter, preferably unsalted

Cracked black peppercorns, to garnish

Fresh herb sprigs, to garnish

FOR THE VEGETABLES
(all, or a selection, of these depending on availability)

1 red pepper

1 yellow pepper

100 ml (3½ fl oz) light olive oil

1 courgette

1 aubergine

1 red onion

1–2 globe artichokes, trimmed

3 small leeks, split and washed

6 large mushroom caps

100 ml (3½ fl oz) extra-virgin olive oil

50 ml (2 fl oz) balsamic vinegar

1 tablespoon chopped fresh thyme

1 tablespoon chopped fresh parsley

1 tablespoon chopped fresh basil

First prepare the vegetables. Rub the peppers with a little of the light olive oil and roast them under a very hot grill or in a very hot oven until the skins are blistering and black. Peel, seed and cut each pepper into six pieces.

Slice the courgette and aubergine into 1 cm (½ in) slices and drizzle lightly with more of the light olive oil. Cut the onion and artichoke into wedges and brush with the oil. Blanch the leeks in a saucepan of boiling, salted water for 2 minutes and then refresh under cold water. Drain thoroughly and brush with a little of the light olive oil. Rub the mushrooms caps with a little of the oil.

Preheat the grill or barbecue and grill all the vegetables until just cooked. The peppers and leeks will only need 1–2 minutes, while the mushroom caps, onion, artichokes, aubergine and courgette will need closer to 5 minutes. Place the vegetables in a ceramic dish and drizzle with the extra-virgin olive oil. This can be done ahead of time. Just a few minutes before serving, drizzle with the balsamic vinegar and sprinkle on the herbs.

To prepare the cheese, preheat the grill to high. To cut the cheese neatly, take a mug of boiling water, dip a knife into it and then cut a slice of the cheese log, about 1.5–2 cm (⅝–¾ in) thick. Repeat until you have four or six neat rounds. Place these rounds flat on a grill rack and butter generously. This helps the cheese brown nicely as it cooks. Place under a hot grill for 2–3 minutes, until nicely browned and heated through.

To serve, place the cheese in the centres of warm plates, and surround with the grilled vegetables. Drizzle the oil and vinegar from the ceramic dish around the vegetables. Garnish with the peppercorns and sprigs of fresh herbs.

smoked salmon with spicy roast onion, on potato bread

This is a real, live 'gourmet-meal-in-minutes' kind of dish. So when you are stuck for a quick starter or a light lunch dish, remember this one!

Serves 4

1 red or white onion

1 tablespoon light olive oil

Salt and freshly ground pepper

$\frac{1}{2}$ teaspoon sugar

A good pinch of chilli powder (or paprika if you don't want it too hot)

4 slices of Potato Bread (see page 229)

2 tablespoons butter

4 large slices of smoked salmon

4 tablespoons crème fraîche, to serve

A few fresh chives, to garnish

Slice the onion into fine wedges.

Heat the olive oil in a frying saucepan over a high heat. Add the onion wedges and season with the salt and pepper, sugar and chilli powder or paprika. Don't cook the onion too much, it should still have a little bite. Drain on kitchen paper.

For a neat presentation, cut rounds out of the potato bread slices with a 10 cm (4 in) round cutter. Toast the rounds lightly on both sides, then butter them while still hot.

Form each slice of smoked salmon into a loose rosette and place on top of the rounds.

Place in the centres of warm plates and top with a dollop of crème fraîche and the roast onions. Garnish with the chives.

sautéed prawns with potato and a basil cream

A simple, quick starter for friends or family, full of fresh ingredients and just bursting with flavour. It works perfectly as a canapé too.

Serves 4

12 large raw king prawns, peeled

FOR THE BASIL CREAM
12 garlic cloves, unpeeled
2 tablespoons butter
2 tablespoons vegetable oil
100 ml (3½ fl oz) cream
Salt and freshly ground pepper
2 waxy potatoes, cooked in their skins
2 tablespoons chopped fresh basil

Preheat the oven to 200°C/400°F/Gas 6.

Make an incision down the rounded backs of the prawns. Remove the intestinal tracts and, with your fingers, press open (butterfly) the prawns slightly. This will give them an attractive shape when cooked.

Prepare the basil cream. Place the cloves of garlic in a saucepan. Cover generously with water and bring to the boil. Boil for just 1 minute and cool under running water. Peel the cloves. Take a sheet of aluminium foil, place the garlic in the centre, and add ½ tablespoon of the butter and ½ tablespoon of the oil. Pull up the corners of the foil to make a small parcel. Place in a baking dish and bake for 30 minutes in the oven.

Boil the cream for 1–2 minutes, until just slightly thickened. Add the garlic and its juices from the foil pack, blend in a food processor and season with salt and pepper. (If you don't have a processor, simply mash the garlic with a fork, and whisk it into the cream.)

Cut the potatoes into a total of 12 even slices and fry in 1 tablespoon of the butter and 1 tablespoon of the oil until golden brown.

Season the prawns to taste. Fry them quickly, over a high heat in the remaining butter and oil, until lightly browned (this takes 20–25 minutes).

To serve, stir the basil into the cream. Place three slices of fried potato on warm plates. Top each slice with a sautéed prawn and surround with the warm sauce. Serve at once.

creamy leek and prawn tart

People just love this tart at our restaurant – we invariably run out every time it is on the menu. We serve it warm with a small salad.

Serves 6

225 g (8 oz) Savoury Shortcrust Pastry
(see page 234)

FOR THE FILLING

25 g (1 oz) unsalted butter

1½ teaspoons salt

200 g (8 oz) leeks, washed, trimmed and
finely sliced

200 g (8 oz) peeled cooked prawns
or shrimps

3 eggs

3 egg yolks

350 ml (12 fl oz) whipping cream

3 tablespoons tomato ketchup

1 tablespoon chopped fresh herbs, such
as parsley, tarragon, chives or basil

A pinch of freshly ground white pepper

Preheat the oven to 180°C/350°F/Gas 4. Roll out the pastry and use it to line a 20 cm (8 in) flan tin. Place in the fridge to chill for at least 20 minutes.

Cover the pastry with foil and line with baking beans. Bake blind (see page 235) in the oven for about 15 minutes until light golden brown. Remove the foil and beans and set the tart case aside to cool.

Reduce the oven temperature to 150°C/300°F/Gas 2.

To cook the leeks, melt the butter in a saucepan with 100 ml (3½ fl oz) of water and ½ teaspoon of salt. Add the leeks and fry gently for about 4–5 minutes until just cooked. Allow the leeks to cool slightly and then squeeze out the excess liquid. Pat the prawns (or shrimps) dry on kitchen paper and mix them with the leeks.

In a medium-sized bowl, whisk together the eggs and egg yolks until well blended. Add the remaining ingredients and the remaining salts and whisk gently until the mixture is smooth. Stir in the prawn and leek mixture.

Gently pour the filling into the tart case and cook in the preheated oven for about 40 minutes, or until completely set. Allow to cool slightly before serving.

seafood bruschetta on irish soda bread, with spring onion butter

Years ago we would have served this buttery seafood in a tartlet shell or on pasta, and of course that would still be delicious today. Nowadays though, to serve it on soft soda farls somehow seems right, so right we wonder why we hadn't thought of it years ago.

Serves 4

2 Irish Soda Farls (see page 228)

1 small bunch of spring onions, washed and trimmed

140 g (5 oz) unsalted butter, cut into 1 cm (½ in) dice

450 g (1 lb) mixed seafood, such as large prawns, peeled and their intestinal tracts removed, smoked haddock, cod, salmon, trimmed and cut into 2 cm (¾ in) dice, or monkfish fillet, trimmed and cut into 3 cm (¼ in) strips

140 g (5 oz) live mussels, washed and debearded (discard any that are open or do not close when tapped)

125 ml (4 fl oz) dry white wine

Salt and freshly ground pepper

2 plum tomatoes, peeled, seeded and roughly diced

2 tablespoons snipped fresh chives

3 tablespoons whipping cream (optional)

A few chervil sprigs, to garnish

Slice the soda farls in half horizontally and then cut into rounds with a 10 cm (4 in) cutter. Place on a tray ready for toasting. Preheat the grill to high.

Finely chop the bottom 4 cm (1½ in) of the spring onions. Place in a large frying saucepan over a moderate heat with 1 tablespoon of the butter, cover and sweat for 1 minute.

Cut the remainder of the spring onions into 4 cm (1½ in) pieces and set aside.

Add all the prawns, fish and mussels to the frying pan and turn the heat up to high. Fry for about a minute and then add the wine, the remaining spring onions and a little salt. Cover and cook just until the mussels are open (discard any that do not open) and then add the tomatoes, chives and the cream, if using, and the remaining butter. Shake the saucepan gently to incorporate all the butter into the sauce.

Toast the farls and place one in the centre of four warm plates. Spoon the fish and seafood generously over with some of the sauce. Garnish with a few sprigs of chervil and serve at once.

brown soda bread and goats' cheese stacks

This is not so much a recipe as an idea for a posh snack. Be careful when making the soda bread croutons – if you let them get too dry they'll break your teeth... well almost!

Serves 4

1 loaf of unsliced brown soda bread

2 tablespoons butter, melted

250 g (9 oz) soft goats' cheese

4–6 small cooked beetroot, cut into 1 cm (½ in) dice

1 tablespoon chopped fresh parsley

4 tablespoons roughly chopped walnuts, lightly toasted

6 tablespoons Vinaigrette Dressing (see page 85)

Salt and freshly ground pepper

1 avocado, peeled, stoned and cut into 1 cm (½ in) dice

125 g (4½ oz) wild rocket

Preheat the oven to 190°C/375°F/Gas 5.

Cut eight very thin slices (about 3 mm or ⅛ in) from the loaf (this is much easier if the loaf is one or two days old). Lay the slices on a baking sheet, and brush one side lightly with the melted butter. Bake until the slices are lightly browned, but be careful not to let them dry out or they will be very tough.

Divide the goats' cheese attractively between the slices of bread. This will be easy if you use small goats' cheese logs, which can be sliced neatly. Alternatively, if using the tub type, spoon out little egg-like shapes, like quenelles.

Toss the beetroot with the parsley, walnuts, 4 tablespoons of the vinaigrette and a little salt and pepper.

To serve, pop the goats' cheese croutons into the oven for just long enough to warm through, about a minute. Place a slice in the centre of each plate and top with a spoonful of the beetroot and the diced avocado. Repeat with a second slice, creating a little stack, again adding beetroot and avocado. It is okay if some of this tumbles onto the plate.

Toss the rocket with the remaining vinaigrette and decorate each plate with a small stack of salad. Serve at once.

smoked salmon carpaccio with a horseradish cream

This is not a classic carpaccio, but borrows the term to define the presentation. We think it's fun, and it certainly looks and tastes wonderful.

Serves 4

300 g (10 oz) thinly sliced smoked salmon

FOR THE HORSERADISH CREAM

2–3 tablespoons whipping cream

2 tablespoons creamed horseradish

1 teaspoon Dijon mustard

1/2 teaspoon sugar

Salt and freshly ground white pepper

TO SERVE

1 small avocado, peeled, stoned and cut into 1 cm (1/2 in) dice and tossed in 1 tablespoon lemon juice

1 cooked beetroot, cut into 1 cm (1/2 in) dice

1 tablespoon snipped fresh chives

1 tablespoon chopped fresh dill

Trim the smoked salmon of any dark pieces. Carefully spread the slices into neat circles to fill the centres of four plates.

To make the horseradish cream, bring the cream to the boil in a small saucepan. Remove from the heat completely and stir in the creamed horseradish, mustard, sugar and a little salt and pepper.

To serve, carefully sprinkle each plate of salmon with a little of the diced avocado and beetroot, pour on some of the horseradish cream and then scatter the herbs over the top.

potato torte with cabbage, bacon and cheddar

This tasty torte can be a luncheon dish in its own right served with a green salad, or it can be used as an accompaniment to grilled meats.

Serves 8

½ Savoy cabbage, outer leaves removed, cored and finely sliced

200 g (8 oz) streaky bacon, cut into 1 cm (½ in) pieces

25 g (1 oz) butter

700 g (1lb 9 oz) potatoes

Salt and freshly ground black pepper

200 g (8 oz) Cheddar cheese, grated

Green salad, to serve

Preheat the oven to 200°C/400°F/Gas 6.

Cook the cabbage in boiling, salted water for 2 minutes. Refresh in cold water and dry thoroughly.

Sauté the bacon in the butter in a heavy frying pan over a medium heat until the bacon is just starting to brown. Remove the bacon from the fat. Reserve the fat, and toss the bacon with the cabbage.

Peel the potatoes and cut into 5 mm (¼ in) slices. Rinse and dry the slices. Season them lightly with salt and pepper and toss them in the bacon fat.

Take a non-stick pan or baking dish, arrange a layer of potatoes on the bottom, and sprinkle lightly with some of the Cheddar. Top this with a layer of cabbage and bacon, and again sprinkle lightly with cheese. Continue building the torte in this fashion until all the ingredients are used up, ending with a layer of potatoes and cheese. It is important that you sprinkle each layer with cheese, as this helps to hold the torte together. Cover with a circle of greaseproof paper and bake in the oven for 45 minutes or until the potatoes are tender when pricked with a knife. Remove from the oven and allow to cool to room temperature.

Remove the greaseproof paper, and turn the torte out onto a cutting board. Carefully cut into eight portions with a sharp knife, and serve each portion on a medium-sized plate with some green salad.

creamy baked pasta with four cheeses

This dish is great for using the leftovers from a cheese board, as you really only need a small amount of each cheese. Without a doubt, Irish cheeses hold their own against any others, so, if you haven't yet tried them, now is the time.

Serves 4

450 g (1 lb) dried macaroni or penne

100 g (4 oz) Cashel Blue or other blue cheese, crumbled

100 g (4 oz) Ring Farmhouse or Irish Cheddar cheese, grated

100 g (4 oz) Cooleeney or Irish Camembert type cheese, sliced

100 g (4 oz) Gabriel, Coolea or Parmesan cheese, grated

100 g (4 oz) butter, plus extra for greasing

4 tablespoons light olive oil

200 g (8 oz) tender young spinach leaves

Salt and freshly ground black pepper

350 g (12 oz) button mushrooms, quartered

2 tablespoons plain white flour

500 ml (18 fl oz) milk

300 ml (½ pint) double cream

Preheat the oven to 190ºC/375ºF/Gas 5.

Grease a large ovenproof baking dish. Bring a large saucepan of salted water to the boil and cook the pasta according to the packet instructions.

Combine the four cheeses in a bowl and set aside.

Heat 25 g (1 oz) of the butter and half the oil in a large frying saucepan over a high heat. Add the spinach, season generously and cook for 2–4 minutes, stirring occasionally, until wilted. Tip into a sieve set over a bowl. When the spinach has cooled a little, squeeze out any excess liquid gently, using your hands.

Place 25 g (1 oz) of the butter and the remaining oil in a large frying saucepan over a medium heat and cook the mushrooms for 2–3 minutes. Season.

Place the remaining butter in a saucepan with the flour and milk and bring to the boil, whisking constantly. Reduce the heat and cook, stirring frequently, for 5–10 minutes, until the sauce is smooth and thickened. Season to taste and stir in the cream.

Drain the pasta and refresh under cold water. Return to the saucepan and add the spinach, mushrooms, white sauce and two-thirds of the cheeses. Toss well until combined. Check for seasoning.

Tip into the baking dish and top with the remaining cheeses. Bake for 15–20 minutes, until bubbling and lightly golden.

vegetable omelette with goats' cheese and basil

The wonderful thing about omelettes is their versatility. This is basically just an Italian-Irish version of a one-pan omelette, rather like a Spanish omelette, and we normally make it with whatever is on hand, in season or at the market.

Serves 4

1 tablespoon olive oil

2 tablespoons unsalted butter

1 small red onion, finely chopped

1 red pepper, seeded and thinly sliced

Salt and freshly ground black pepper

1 courgette, cut into 2 cm (^{3}/$_4$ in) dice

140 g (5 oz) cooked potatoes, cut into 2 cm (^{3}/$_4$ in) dice

8 eggs, beaten with ^{1}/$_2$ teaspoon salt

140 g (5 oz) goats' cheese log, crumbled

A small handful of fresh basil leaves, torn or chopped

2 tablespoons freshly grated Parmesan cheese

Mixed salad leaves, to garnish

Preheat the grill to high. Heat a large, heavy frying saucepan over a high heat. Add the oil and butter and allow the butter to foam. Add the onion and pepper and a little salt and sauté over a medium-high heat for 3–4 minutes.

Now add the courgette and potatoes. If the saucepan seems to get very dry or the vegetables begin to stick or brown too much, add a few tablespoons of water. This will stop the vegetables from burning, encourage them to wilt, and prevent the need for more oil. When the vegetables are cooked to your liking, taste for seasoning and add salt and pepper as necessary.

Now stir the eggs gently into the vegetable mixture. Add the goats' cheese and basil and continue stirring the saucepan very gently until the eggs begin to set. Spread the mixture out evenly over the pan, press it down gently, and sprinkle with the Parmesan.

Place the saucepan underneath the hot grill until the omelette is glazed and slightly puffed. Allow it to rest in the saucepan for a few minutes, then turn out onto a warm serving plate and divide into four equal portions. Serve the omelette garnished with a few salad leaves.

Jeanne's first salad in Ireland stands out in her memory. There was some grated carrot, cut up cooked beets, some cabbage in mayonnaise, a sliced tomato and a little shredded butter lettuce, all in neat little piles with no dressing. It was all very tasty and fresh, but she remembers thinking, don't the Irish know anything about salads? Well, that was eons ago, and nowadays the Irish are definitely coming to grips with the concept of salads.

Personally, we adore salads, especially 'compound' ones — the type that have a multitude of ingredients, and not only vegetables. We find they are great for entertaining, for lunches, dinner parties, buffets, late-night snacks, and so on and so on. We love to take classic Irish combinations and turn them into salads. Just take a look at the Warm Salad of Fish and Chips or our Salad of Bacon and Egg with Crunchy Croutons (see pages 76 and 84). And we love the Wilted Cabbage Salad with Bacon and Cashel Blue Cheese and the Summer Salad Roscoff (see pages 67 and 70).

Smoked products are also fantastic in salads. Their intensity of flavour lends itself well to blending and harmonizing with other ingredients. We offer up versions with Irish smoked eel, smoked pheasant and smoked salmon.

Last, but by no means least, Irish seafood, cooked quickly and simply, can lift a salad into the realm of an unforgettable meal. Try the Lobster Salad with Basil Mayonnaise or the Prawn, Avocado and Tomato Cocktail (see pages 72 and 82), both are slightly modern versions of favourite oldies.

As you can see, we don't think of salads as mere accompaniments, and neither will you once you try a couple from this chapter.

salads

warm potato and black pudding salad

This is a simple meat and two veg salad, which can be served as a tasty starter or a satisfying lunch dish. Feel free to substitute sausages for the black pudding if you prefer, but the version that we give here does have more dramatic colour.

Serves 6

12 small waxy potatoes, unpeeled

175 ml (6 fl oz) Vinaigrette Dressing (see page 85)

2 shallots, finely diced

1 tablespoon chopped fresh parsley

Salt and freshly ground black pepper

1½ tablespoons vegetable oil

450 g (1 lb) black pudding, cut into 1 cm (½ in) slices

350 g (12 oz) broccoli florets

6 tablespoons meat gravy (optional), to serve

1½ tablespoons snipped fresh chives, to serve

Place the potatoes in a small pan, cover with lightly salted water, bring to the boil, and simmer over a medium-high heat until tender. Drain and allow to cool slightly. Peel the potatoes and cut into 5 mm (¼ in) slices. In a small bowl, toss the potatoes in the vinaigrette, with the shallots and parsley. Season with a little salt and pepper.

Heat a large frying saucepan over a moderate heat and add the oil and sliced black pudding. Fry the slices for 3 minutes on each side. Add to the potatoes.

While the black pudding is cooking, bring a saucepan of lightly salted water to the boil, and drop in the broccoli florets. Cook for 4 minutes. Drain thoroughly and add to the potatoes.

To serve, gently toss the potatoes, black pudding and broccoli together. Spoon onto warmed plates. Finish with a spoonful of warmed gravy, if using, and the snipped chives.

wilted cabbage salad with bacon and cashel blue cheese

A warm, wintry salad with savoury flavours that entice and win over even those who think they don't like cabbage. You can use another blue cheese if you can't find Cashel.

Serves 6

3 slices of plain bread, cut into 1 cm (1/2 in) cubes

6 tablespoons duck or goose fat

200 g (8 oz) streaky bacon, cut into 5 cm (2 in) pieces

1 garlic clove, chopped

3 tablespoons red wine vinegar

Salt and freshly ground black pepper

1 Savoy cabbage, thick ribs removed and leaves sliced

1/2 head of radicchio, thinly sliced

200 g (8 oz) Cashel Blue cheese, crumbled

Preheat the oven to 180°C/350°F/Gas 4.

Toss the bread cubes in 2 tablespoons of the duck or goose fat and bake for approximately 10 minutes, tossing and turning frequently. They should be brown and crusty.

To make the dressing, sauté the bacon pieces in 2 tablespoons of the fat in a large frying pan over a moderate heat, until the bacon is beginning to crisp nicely. Remove the bacon with a slotted spoon, add the garlic and let it fry gently for 1 minute.

Remove from the heat and carefully add the vinegar. Scrape the bottom of the pan to loosen any caramelized juices. Taste the hot dressing for salt and add some freshly ground pepper.

To wilt the cabbage, heat a very large frying pan with the remaining fat over a moderate heat. Add the cabbage all at once. Cook, stirring for about 1½ minutes. Then tip into a large bowl.

To serve, combine the radicchio, bacon, cheese and croutons with the warm cabbage and toss with the dressing. Arrange each portion on a warm plate by spooning the mixture into a 10 cm (4 in) cookie cutter or cooking ring and pressing down slightly until the cabbage mixture forms a neat shape. Carefully remove the ring and serve at once.

salad of artichoke, country ham, leek, peas and egg

We tend to use this as a main-course lunch salad at the restaurant, and often serve a whole artichoke per person. Artichokes are a vegetable that some people just don't 'get' and yet others, like ourselves, would order them every time we came across them. The simplest way to get to know and love artichokes is to steam them whole, then eat them with some melted butter, leaf by leaf (but not the tips of the outside leaves) – divine.

Serves 6

Salt and pepper

2 leeks, washed, trimmed and finely sliced

4 heaped tablespoons fresh or thawed frozen peas

6 fresh free-range organic eggs

Mixed salad leaves

100 ml (3½ fl oz) Vinaigrette Dressing (see page 85)

6 medium slices of cooked country ham or gammon, cut into 1 cm (½ in) strips

2 tablespoons snipped fresh chives, to garnish

Fresh chervil or dill sprigs, to garnish

FOR THE ARTICHOKES

2 tablespoons olive oil

2 tablespoons white wine vinegar

1 tablespoon salt

3 medium globe artichokes

First cook the artichokes. Mix the oil, vinegar and salt with 1 litre (1¾ pints) of water in a saucepan. Carefully trim the outside leaves from the artichokes with a very sharp knife, until you are left with only the artichoke hearts. Simmer the artichoke hearts in the cooking liquid for about 20 minutes or until they are just tender. Allow them to cool in the liquid, then use a spoon to scoop out the hairy chokes at the centre. Cut each heart into about ten wedges and reserve in a little of the cooking liquid.

Bring about 150 ml (¼ pint) of water to the boil in a saucepan, and add a little salt. Add the leeks and peas and cook for about 1 minute. Drain and allow to cool on a plate.

Boil the eggs for 6–7 minutes, then cool in cold water. Peel carefully under running water. Carefully cut each egg into four and reserve on a plate.

To serve, toss the salad leaves with a little of the vinaigrette dressing and arrange in a bed on each plate. Season the leeks and peas with a little salt and pepper, and a little of the vinaigrette, and scatter over the salad. Divide the eggs, artichoke wedges, and ham slices between the plates and garnish with the snipped chives and chervil or dill sprigs.

summer salad roscoff

This salad is inspired by the famous salade Niçoise. We are sure that if the people of Provence were to spend time in Ireland, they would wholeheartedly approve of our substituting salmon for tuna.

Serves 4

200 ml (8 fl oz) white wine

2 tablespoons white wine vinegar

1 bouquet garni

1 teaspoon salt

450 g (1 lb) salmon fillet, any remaining bones removed

FOR THE SALAD GARNISHES

125 g (4½ oz) green beans, cut into 2 cm (¾ in) lengths

TO SERVE

120 g (4½ oz) mixed salad leaves

4 tablespoons Vinaigrette Dressing (see page 85)

½ cucumber, peeled, quartered lengthways and diced

250 g (9 oz) tasty salad tomatoes

4 eggs, hard-boiled for 9 minutes, peeled and quartered

12 black olives, stoned

FOR THE ANCHOVY AND BASIL DRESSING

4 tablespoons Mayonnaise (see page 232)

1 tablespoon chopped fresh basil

2 anchovy fillets, finely minced

Salt and freshly ground black pepper

To cook the salmon, pour the wine, vinegar and 200 ml (7 fl oz) of water into a saucepan wide enough to take the salmon fillet. Add the bouquet garni and salt and bring to the boil. Immerse the salmon in the liquid and simmer very gently for 2 minutes. Remove from the heat, cover and allow to cool.

Cook the green beans in boiling, salted water for 6 minutes and then drain. Refresh in cold water and drain again.

To make the anchovy and basil dressing, whisk the mayonnaise, chopped basil and minced anchovies together in a small bowl. Thin with 2 tablespoons of the salmon poaching liquid, whisking continually. Taste for seasoning, and add salt and pepper as needed.

To serve, toss the salad leaves with the vinaigrette dressing. Arrange them attractively in the centre of each plate. Arrange the remaining salad ingredients around the salad leaves. Remove the salmon from the poaching liquid and flake carefully onto each plate. Drizzle with some of the anchovy and basil dressing.

salad of smoked eel with beetroot and chive cream

Good smoked eel is a really great product that is well worth trying. Buy it whole, in its skin, to ensure freshness.

Serves 4

2 uncooked beetroot, trimmed

1 tablespoon Dijon mustard

150 ml (¼ pint) Vinaigrette Dressing (see page 85)

Salt and freshly ground pepper

1 smoked eel (whole, skin on)

1 tablespoon lemon juice

4 tablespoons cream

A small bunch of chives, snipped

Mixed salad leaves, to serve

If you have a microwave, wrap the beetroot in clingfilm and microwave at full power for about 12 minutes. Otherwise you can boil the beetroot in water for 30–60 minutes until tender, depending on size. Unwrap the beetroot and, with kitchen paper, simply push the skins off. Cut into neat 5 mm (¼ in) slices.

Whisk the mustard into the vinaigrette dressing and marinate the beetroot slices with a little salt and pepper in half of this vinaigrette mixture for at least 30 minutes.

To prepare the eel, pull the head back, breaking the backbone at the neck. Pull the head towards the tail, to free the skin and pull it off. Now run a small knife down both sides of the backbone. Prise the flesh away from the bone with your fingers, releasing any tricky bits with your knife. Cut the fillets into 6 cm (2½ in) pieces and set aside.

Mix the lemon juice with the cream, chives and a little salt and pepper.

To serve, toss the salad leaves with some of the remaining vinaigrette and arrange them in the centre of each plate. Arrange the beetroot in three piles around the salad, and place pieces of smoked eel in between these piles. Drizzle each plate generously with the chive cream.

lobster salad with basil mayonnaise

This is an old favourite that we never tire of and which never fails to draw compliments. Freeze the leftover shells and use them for a lobster stock, or fill them with the lobster mayonnaise for a really dramatic presentation.

Serves 4

2 live lobsters, weighing about 500 g (1 lb 2 oz)

FOR THE BASIL MAYONNAISE

1 tablespoon white wine vinegar

1 tablespoon Dijon mustard

3 egg yolks

½ teaspoon salt

6 tablespoons chopped fresh basil

500 ml (18 fl oz) vegetable oil or light olive oil

TO SERVE

Mixed salad leaves

2 tablespoons Vinaigrette Dressing (see page 85)

6 yellow cherry tomatoes, halved

6 red cherry tomatoes, halved

1 avocado, peeled, stoned and sliced

First make the basil mayonnaise. Blend the vinegar, mustard, egg yolks and salt until the salt is dissolved. Add the basil and, while the food processor is running, add the oil in a slow steady stream, until it has completely emulsified into a thick mayonnaise.

To kill the lobsters, place each one on a board and cover it with foil and a cloth. Hold firmly down with one hand and, with the point of large knife, pierce down to the board through the cross on the centre of the head.

Bring a saucepan of salted water to a vigorous boil. Put the lobsters in and cook for 12 minutes. Then stop the cooking process by plunging the lobsters into a basin of cold water. When they are cool enough to handle, pull the claws from the bodies. Crack the claws and remove the meat. With a large chef's knife cut each lobster in half from the back, along the length of its body, and remove its intestinal tract. Remove the tail meat and slice it up neatly, along with the claw meat. Reserve the lobster meat and the body shells.

To serve, toss the salad leaves in the vinaigrette dressing and pile in the centres of four plates. Surround in an attractive manner with the cherry tomatoes, avocado slices and finally the lobster meat. Spoon the mayonnaise onto each plate, either in one dollop or, if you prefer, drizzled over the lobster and salad. Serve immediately.

warm salad of sautéed chicken livers with sliced potatoes, hazelnuts and green beans

Soaking the chicken livers in milk will remove any unpleasant, bitter tastes. Keep them pink in the middle so that they retain their silky texture.

Serves 4

500 g (1 lb 2 oz) chicken livers
250 ml (9 fl oz) milk
Salt and freshly ground pepper
4 tablespoons butter

FOR THE HAZELNUT VINAIGRETTE
1 teaspoon Dijon mustard
30 ml (1 fl oz) white wine vinegar
Salt and freshly ground white pepper
100 ml (3½ fl oz) hazelnut oil
50 ml (2 fl oz) light olive oil

FOR THE SALAD
140 g (5 oz) baby salad potatoes, unpeeled
Salt and freshly ground pepper
100 g (4 oz) fine green beans
2 spring onions, finely chopped
1 tablespoon hazelnuts, roasted and chopped

To prepare the chicken livers, trim off any sinews and green bile spots. Soak the livers in the milk for at least a couple of hours (ideally overnight).

To make the hazelnut vinaigrette, in a small bowl whisk the mustard, vinegar and salt and pepper to taste until the salt is dissolved. Slowly add the oils, whisking constantly. Check the seasoning and adjust if necessary.

To prepare the salad, boil the potatoes in boiling, salted water, then refresh them in cold water. Peel the skins off, if you wish, and slice into rounds. Season with salt and pepper. Drizzle with some of the hazelnut vinaigrette and keep in a warm place.

Cook the beans in boiling, salted water for about 6 minutes, then refresh them in plenty of cold water. Drain and cut into 1 cm (½ in) lengths. Season with salt and pepper. Add the chopped spring onions, the hazelnuts and a few tablespoons of the hazelnut vinaigrette. Don't add the vinaigrette too far in advance or the beans will lose their bright green colour.

To sauté the chicken livers, take the livers out of the milk and drain them on kitchen paper. Season generously with salt and pepper. Heat the butter in a large frying saucepan over a high heat until the butter is foaming. Add the livers in one layer and allow them to brown, without shaking them, for about 3 minutes. Turn them over and cook for 1 minute. The livers should remain slightly pink inside.

To serve, spoon the sliced potatoes onto the centres of four plates and surround with the green bean mixture. Put the livers on top of the potatoes and serve at once.

orzo pasta salad with tomatoes and mushrooms

Okay, this may not sound very Irish, but in fact, in the right season we have gorgeous home-grown tomatoes and mushrooms. Orzo is a nice size pasta for salad; it keeps a good bite and mixes well with the other ingredients.

Serves 6

225 g (8 oz) orzo

280 g (10 oz) mushrooms, quartered or sliced

6 tablespoons finely chopped onion

3 tablespoons lemon juice

1/2 teaspoon salt

3 tablespoons olive oil

3 ripe tomatoes, peeled, seeded and diced

2 tablespoons chopped fresh parsley

1 tablespoon chopped fresh dill

Salt and freshly ground black pepper

Bring about 3 litres (5¼ pints) of salted water to the boil in a large saucepan. Add the orzo, stir well, then return the water to the boil. Cook the orzo until just al dente. Drain the pasta and refresh under cold running water. Allow to drain well in a colander while you prepare the mushrooms.

Bring 100 ml (3½ fl oz) of water to the boil in a saucepan. Add the mushrooms, onion, lemon juice and salt. Cover and cook for 4 minutes. Allow to cool slightly, then add the oil, tomatoes and herbs.

Combine the orzo with the mushroom mixture in an attractive serving bowl. Check the seasoning and adjust to taste with salt and pepper.

warm salad of fish and chips

This is a favourite lunch dish. The crispy fish and chips are a great contrast to the
salad. This dish also works well as a very elegant starter, so if you feel like it try it with
a slightly fancier presentation.

Serves 4

1 large baking potato, peeled

Oil for deep frying

Salt

400 g (14 oz) monkfish fillets

1 egg, lightly beaten

100 g (4 oz) plain white flour, seasoned

Mixed salad leaves, to serve

2 tablespoons Vinaigrette Dressing
(see page 85), to serve

FOR THE MUSTARD SAUCE

175 ml (6 fl oz) double cream

2 tablespoons wholegrain mustard

Cut the potato into wafer-thin slices or matchstick-sized sticks. Soak in cold
water for about 1 hour or in a colander under running water for 15 minutes to
remove excess starch.

Preheat the oil in a deep-fat fryer to 190°C/375°F.

Drain the potato slices or sticks and dry well with a tea towel. Fry for about
3–4 minutes or until they are crisp and golden. Drain again on kitchen paper and
season with salt. Set aside.

To make the mustard sauce, reserve 2 tablespoons of the cream and bring the
remainder to the boil in a small saucepan. Simmer for about 1 minute until
slightly thickened. Remove from the heat and whisk in the mustard.

Slice the monkfish fillets into pieces about 1 cm (½ in) thick. Whisk together
the egg and the reserved cream and rub this vigorously into the monkfish pieces.
Dredge the pieces in the flour, pushing the flour into the pieces so that it
absorbs all the cream and egg mixture.

Deep-fry the monkfish in the hot oil (again at 190°C/375°F) for 3 minutes, or
until crisp and golden. Remove and drain on kitchen paper.

Toss the salad leaves in the vinaigrette dressing and divide between four
plates. Top the salad leaves with the fish pieces and the chips. Drizzle with the
mustard sauce and serve at once.

seared beef salad with cashel blue dressing

This is a gorgeous salad so we reckon you ought to try it. Now, if you like it you should also try the 'mother' version that it came from: use Parmesan cheese instead of the Cashel Blue, add a few drops of truffle oil to the celery, and serve with a rocket salad instead of mixed leaves. It is a sort of Italian cousin to this one.

Serves 4

350 g (12 oz) beef fillet, trimmed and in one piece

1 tablespoon olive oil

½ teaspoon salt

1 teaspoon cracked black peppercorns

Mixed salad leaves, to serve

1 tablespoon snipped fresh chives, to garnish

Fresh chervil leaves, to garnish

FOR THE CELERY

3 celery sticks, cut diagonally into 1 cm (½ in) slices

3 tablespoons olive oil

¼ teaspoon salt

½ teaspoon cracked black peppercorns

FOR THE CASHEL BLUE DRESSING

50 g (2 oz) Cashel Blue cheese, crumbled

150 ml (¼ pint) Vinaigrette Dressing (see page 85)

Make sure that the beef fillet is trimmed and free of sinew and fat. Cut in half lengthways so that you have two longish, flat pieces. Season these with the olive oil, salt and peppercorns.

Heat a cast-iron frying saucepan over a very high heat until very hot. Add the beef and cook for 2 minutes on each side for rare, and about 5 minutes on each side for medium to well done. When cooked, transfer the beef to a plate, and allow to cool.

To cook the celery, place in a small saucepan with the other ingredients and 150 ml (¼ pint) of water. Cover tightly and simmer for 4 minutes. Remove the saucepan from the heat and allow the celery to cook in the liquid.

To make the Cashel Blue dressing, simply whisk the crumbled cheese with the vinaigrette dressing in a small bowl.

To serve, slice the beef thinly and arrange on four plates, with a little celery. Place the salad leaves in the centre of each and spoon on a little dressing. Garnish with the chives and chervil leaves.

smoked pheasant salad with lentils and roast garlic

Smoked game and poultry are excellent and versatile products. Try this salad with smoked chicken, duck, or even turkey. Keep any bones for stock, and use it when making your next batch of celery or lentil soup.

Serves 4

125 g (4½ oz) green lentils
2 tablespoons chopped carrots
2 tablespoons chopped onion
2 tablespoons chopped leeks
1 fresh parsley sprig
1½ teaspoons dried thyme
1 head of garlic
200 ml (7 fl oz) olive oil
600 ml (1 pint) cream
1 smoked pheasant
Salt and freshly ground pepper
200 ml (8 fl oz) Vinaigrette Dressing (see page 85)
Mixed salad leaves, to serve
125 g (4½ oz) cooked green beans, diced, to serve

Place the lentils and water to cover in a large saucepan, bring to the boil, and simmer for 5 minutes, skimming the scum that comes to the surface. Add the carrots, onion, leeks, parsley and thyme and simmer for 20 minutes.

Preheat the oven to 120°C/250°F/Gas ½.

Separate the cloves of garlic by putting the head in a saucepan of cold water. Bring to the boil, and simmer for 5 minutes. Then refresh under cold water. Peel the cloves, put in a heavy ovenproof pan with the oil and slowly roast in the oven for approximately 1 hour.

Drain the lentils and add the cream and three cloves of the garlic.

Take the meat off the smoked pheasant carcass. Slice the breast meat thinly and dice the leg meat. Arrange the meat on a baking tray and season with salt and pepper and a little of the vinaigrette dressing. Pop the pheasant into the preheated oven to warm slightly.

Toss the salad leaves lightly in the remaining vinaigrette and arrange in the centres of the plates. Spoon some of the creamed lentils around the leaves and sprinkle the beans and the remaining roast garlic cloves on the lentils. Take the warmed pheasant and arrange it attractively on top of the salad. Serve while the lentils and pheasant are still warm.

smoked salmon extravaganza

This is a carefully composed salad that is a feast to behold. All the ingredients have been put together to complement each other both visually and in terms of flavour. Feel free to substitute ingredients, but think about how this will affect the whole dish.

Serves 6

350 g (12 oz) smoked salmon slices
225 g (8 oz) rocket leaves
4 ripe tomatoes, peeled and sliced
1 cucumber
1 small red onion, thinly sliced
4 eggs, hard-boiled for 9 minutes and shelled
1 tablespoon snipped fresh chives
1 tablespoon chive flowers
12 nasturtium flowers, to garnish
Fresh chervil and dill sprigs, to garnish

FOR THE CREAMY DILL DRESSING
4 tablespoons lemon juice
2 teaspoons Dijon mustard
$\frac{1}{2}$ teaspoon salt
$\frac{1}{2}$ teaspoon white pepper
300 ml ($\frac{1}{2}$ pint) whipping cream, chilled
3 tablespoons chopped fresh dill

First make the creamy dill dressing. Whisk together the lemon juice, mustard, salt and pepper in a small bowl. Stir in the cream and chopped dill. Taste for seasoning.

Cut away any dark flesh from the salmon slices using a small sharp knife. Arrange the slices along the middle of a large serving platter, rolling and folding them into attractive curves. Arrange the rocket leaves all around the edges of the platter. Next, lay the tomato slices on both sides of the salmon, but sitting on the stems of the rocket leaves to help keep them in place.

Peel the cucumber, cut it in half lengthwise, and scoop out the seeds with a teaspoon. Cut each half into thin slices. Lay the cucumber inside the tomato slices, next to the smoked salmon. Sprinkle the onion slices over the tomatoes and cucumber. Roughly chop the egg yolks and whites separately. Sprinkle the yolks over the rocket, and the whites over the smoked salmon. Sprinkle the chives and chive flowers over the salmon. Finally, scatter the nasturtium flowers and sprigs of herbs where you feel they look best. To serve, sprinkle generously with the creamy dill dressing.

prawn, avocado and tomato cocktail

Here we have a very simple but perfect little prawn or shrimp cocktail – you can make it with either. We like to present it in small cos leaves that look like little boats. It would make a smashing canapé.

Serves 4

350 g (12 oz) peeled cooked prawns or shrimps

1 avocado, peeled, stoned and cut into 1cm (½ in) dice

8 red cherry tomatoes, quartered

8 yellow cherries tomatoes, quartered

Salt and freshly ground black pepper

12 small green lettuce leaves, such as cos lettuce

Fresh coriander sprigs, to garnish

FOR THE SAUCE

6 tablespoons natural yoghurt

6 tablespoons Mayonnaise (see page 232)

2 tablespoons tomato ketchup

½ teaspoon chilli powder

2 tablespoons chopped fresh coriander

First make the sauce. Whisk together all the ingredients in a small bowl. If you are making the sauce in advance, don't add the coriander until the last moment. Without the herb, the sauce will keep for 4–5 days in the fridge.

To assemble, gently toss together the prawns or shrimps with the avocado, tomatoes, and half the sauce. Add a little salt and some pepper. Now trim the main rib on the back of each salad leaf so that it will sit on a plate without rolling over. Put a spoonful of the remaining sauce on each plate. Fill each salad leaf with the prawn or shrimp mixture and arrange three leaves on each plate. Garnish each with a sprig of coriander and serve.

rice salad with grilled red onion, peppers and fresh coriander

Rice salads are great in concept, but frequently terribly disappointing. This one, however, is packed full of flavour since the peppers and onions are chargrilled on the barbecue, then chopped and thrown in at the last minute.

Serves 6

300 g (10 oz) long-grain rice

6 tablespoons Vinaigrette Dressing
(see page 85)

2 large red chillies, seeded and
finely chopped

3 tablespoons chopped fresh coriander

Salt and freshly ground black pepper

1 red onion

1 tablespoon olive oil

1 small yellow pepper

1 small red pepper

Preheat the barbecue. Cook the rice in plenty of boiling, salted water, following the directions on the packet, until just tender. Drain and refresh under plenty of cold water. Pat the rice dry in a clean cloth, then place in a serving bowl. Stir in the vinaigrette dressing, chillies and coriander. Check and adjust the seasoning to taste.

Slice the onion into 4–5 thick slices, season with a little salt and pepper and rub with the oil. When the barbecue coals are flaming (but not glowing), put the peppers on its grill until their skins are quite charred. Now add the onion slices and grill for about 2 minutes on each side. Remove the vegetables and, when they are cool enough to handle, peel and seed the peppers and cut them into fine dice. Then finely dice the red onion slices. Add to the rice salad, and serve.

salad of bacon and egg, with crunchy croutons

What a perfect light, lunchy, brunchy sort of dish! Don't just save it for special occasions though, it'll be loved as a quick dinner dish as well.

Serves 4

FOR THE CROUTONS

1 tablespoon light olive oil

1 tablespoon butter

4 slices of stale bread, cut into 1 cm (½ in) cubes

FOR THE DRESSING

1 tablespoon light olive oil

8–12 slices of streaky bacon, cut into even-sized pieces

1 garlic clove, finely chopped

350 ml (12 fl oz) white wine vinegar

Freshly ground black pepper

FOR THE POACHED EGGS

4 tablespoons wine vinegar

1 tablespoon salt

Mixed salad leaves, to serve

4 very fresh free-range organic eggs

FOR THE MUSTARD SAUCE

4 tablespoons Mayonnaise (see page 232)

½ tablespoon wholegrain mustard

Make the croutons. Heat a large frying saucepan over a medium-high heat. Add the oil and butter and allow to melt. Add the bread cubes and toss quickly to coat evenly. Cook gently over a low heat for 5–10 minutes, until the bread is crisp and lightly browned. Drain on kitchen paper and set aside.

To make the dressing, place a large frying saucepan over medium heat again. Add the tablespoon of oil and the bacon. Cook until golden and lightly crisp. Take the saucepan off the heat and add the garlic. Allow to cook for 30 seconds. Add the vinegar, being careful that your saucepan is not too hot, or it will splutter. Shake the saucepan to mix the vinegar with the fat and the bacon juices. This will be a delicious dressing. Add a little pepper, and set to one side while you poach the eggs.

Next make the poached eggs. Fill a tall saucepan with water and bring to the boil. Add the 4 tablespoons vinegar and the 1 tablespoon salt and keep at a very gentle simmer until you are ready to poach the eggs. Carefully break the eggs into four individual saucers or ramekins, being careful not to separate the yolks from the whites. Tip the eggs into the simmering water and simmer until just cooked but still soft on the inside (about 3–4 minutes). Remove from the water with a slotted spoon and trim away any ragged edges of white.

To make the mustard sauce, simply stir together the mayonnaise, mustard and 2 tablespoons of water in a small bowl.

To serve, spread the salad leaves on four warm plates. Sprinkle over the warm bacon pieces with the dressing and croutons, and top each serving with a perfectly poached egg. Finally, drizzle the mustard sauce over and around, and serve at once.

cos salad with blue cheese and walnuts

This is a wonderful alternative to a Caesar salad, especially if you intend to serve it as a first course.

Serves 4

1 large head of cos lettuce
50 g (2 oz) walnuts, toasted

FOR THE DRESSING
2 tablespoons white wine vinegar
1 teaspoon Dijon mustard
¼ teaspoon salt
Freshly ground pepper
60 ml (2¼ fl oz) walnut oil
60 ml (2¼ fl oz) vegetable oil
125 g (4½ oz) blue cheese
(Cashel Blue is ideal)

Trim off any coarse or wilted leaves from the lettuce and cut the head into quarters (on the length, keeping the root on). Wash and dry thoroughly.

The toasted walnuts can be skinned if you wish. You can do this by scraping them with a small pointed knife or by rubbing them in a mesh basket or sieve.

To make the dressing, whisk the vinegar with the mustard, salt and pepper. Then whisk in the oils. Lastly, crumble the cheese into the dressing.

To serve, arrange the lettuce leaves on four plates. Spoon the dressing over them and sprinkle with the walnuts.

vinaigrette dressing

Years ago people used vinaigrettes to dress salads and salads only. But now, realizing that they are tasty, healthy and open to endless variations of flavour, you will find them on vegetables, pastas, fish dishes, and so on. A good ratio to work to is one part vinegar to four or five parts oil. For those with food allergies, a good substitute for vinegar is lemon juice.

Makes about 250 ml (9 fl oz)

½ teaspoon salt
½ teaspoon freshly ground black pepper
2 teaspoons Dijon mustard
2–4 tablespoons white wine vinegar
225 ml (8 fl oz) light olive oil

Dissolve the salt, pepper and mustard in the vinegar in a bowl. Whisk in the oil, slowly at first to allow it to be incorporated. Check and adjust the seasoning to taste.

Alternatively, this dressing can easily be made in a food processor. Simply place all the ingredients in together, and blend.

Remember to keep all vinaigrettes in the fridge if they are not being used immediately, otherwise they can develop a rancid taste.

Fish and shellfish are consistently among the best products that Ireland has on offer, so it's a bit ironic that so many people here say they don't like seafood. The Spanish must think we are absolutely bonkers! People say that is changing though, but sometimes we're not so sure.

When Paul was a lad he loved his local fish and chips and the wild salmon he ate during summer holidays on the Antrim coast. Nowadays, kids seem to prefer burgers and chicken nuggets. It can be hard enough to get them to even taste the likes of fish or shellfish until they are teenagers – we know that for sure (none of our kids will even try any yet).

The good news is that in our restaurants we are selling more seafood than ever. Our customers trust us to source and cook it for them, and even seem more willing to try some of our more unfamiliar products like skate, eel and even razor clams. Of course, they know these items are good for them, but confidence is important with seafood because we all know how stinky and unappealing a bad piece of fish can be. There have been far too many years of heavy sauces masking low-quality products, we think.

Clearly, freshness is the most important factor with seafood. Fresh fish will not smell fishy; in fact, it will smell very clean and kind of salty. It should also be firm and shiny without any tinges of yellow or brown. Most of us know to check the eyes and gills of a whole fish – the eyes should be clear and shiny, the gills should be bright red. But often the way to get the best fish is to find a good fishmonger who will honestly recommend what is good that day; you can learn an awful lot from him.

The most important rule when cooking seafood is not to overcook it. Most fish have quite fragile flesh and overcooking will destroy that completely. Steaming is the most gentle and forgiving method for cooking fish and will leave those delicate flavours and textures intact. Pan-frying is probably the most appealing and popular style of cooking, so if you are keen on fish, invest in a good non-stick frying pan. Deep-fried fish is also delicious of course, but here a careful touch is required to make it work. The temperature of the oil should be approximately 190°C/375°F, and remember not to overcrowd the fryer. Trying to deep-fry too much fish at once will reduce the temperature of the oil significantly and won't allow for even cooking either.

There seem to be so many hints and tips when it comes to seafood. But we don't mean to scare you off. Like all cooking, it is just a matter of getting stuck in and giving it a go. You get a feel for it, and the more you cook seafood, the better you will get.

fish and shellfish

fillets of salmon with a horseradish crust and chive cream sauce

There is a wonderful contrast here between the softness of the cooked salmon and the crisp, spicy crust. This is definitely worth a go at your next dinner party.

Serves 4

750 g (1 lb 10 oz) skinless salmon fillet
Salt and freshly ground pepper
Plain white flour, for dredging
1 tablespoon vegetable oil
1 tablespoon butter
Buttered, cooked vegetables, such as spinach, to serve (optional)

FOR THE CHIVE CREAM SAUCE
250 ml (9 fl oz) double cream
1 teaspoon Dijon mustard
1 teaspoon English mustard
1 teaspoon creamed horseradish
1–2 tablespoons lemon juice
Salt
1 tablespoon snipped fresh chives

FOR THE HORSERADISH CRUST
2 tablespoons creamed horseradish
1 egg yolk
100 g (4 oz) coarse breadcrumbs
1 tablespoon chopped fresh parsley

Preheat the oven to 180°C/350°F/Gas 4.

First make the chive cream sauce. Boil the cream in a saucepan for 2 minutes or until it has thickened slightly. Remove from the heat and whisk in the mustards, horseradish and lemon juice and taste for seasoning, adding a little more salt or lemon juice as necessary. Keep the sauce warm but do not let it boil again or the flavours of the mustard and horseradish will be spoilt.

To prepare the salmon, check that it has been properly trimmed and is boneless. If there are any bones remaining, remove with a pair of tweezers. Cut the salmon into four equal portions. Season each piece with salt and pepper and then dredge lightly with flour.

For the horseradish crust, mix together the horseradish and egg yolk. Dip the top side of each piece of salmon into the horseradish/egg-yolk mixture, making sure that each fillet is generously coated. Mix together the breadcrumbs and parsley and then dip each piece of fish into the breadcrumbs. Shape the crust by pressing this mixture onto the fillets gently but firmly, with your hands.

To cook the salmon, heat the oil in a heavy-based frying pan until very hot. Add the fillets, crust-side down, with the butter and cook for 3 minutes or until the breadcrumbs are beginning to crisp up nicely. Turn the fillets over and finish off the cooking in the oven for 5 minutes.

To serve, add the chives to the sauce. Place each fillet on a warm plate, laying it on a bed of buttered, cooked vegetables if you wish (spinach is a great choice), and surround with a little of the sauce.

perfect salmon with a simple sauce

So many people ask for a recipe for a tasty sauce to go with fish. Well, this is it. It's a base sauce that can be jazzed up with any amount of interesting herbs or flavourings.

Serves 6

1 side of fresh salmon, weighing about 1.5 kg (3 lb 5 oz), skinned and boned

2 tablespoons vegetable oil

Salt and freshly ground white pepper

FOR THE SAUCE

200 g (8 oz) unsalted butter, chilled and diced

2 shallots, finely chopped

250 ml (9 fl oz) dry white wine

100 ml (3½ fl oz) whipping cream

Salt and freshly ground white pepper

First make the sauce. Melt a little of the butter and sweat the shallots for about 2 minutes over a medium heat until they are soft and transparent. Add the wine and boil it quickly until it has reduced to about 4 tablespoons. Pour in the cream and boil again for 1 minute. Reduce the heat to low, and start to whisk in the remaining butter, a tablespoon at a time. Continue to whisk until all the butter has been incorporated. If the sauce seems too thick, add a little water; if it seems too thin, boil it carefully to reduce slightly (you must be very careful if you do this, because the high butter content will cause the sauce to separate easily). Season with salt and pepper and set aside just near the hob, in a warm, but not hot, place.

Ask your fishmonger for a skinless, boneless side of fresh salmon. You should probably order this at least 4 hours before you plan to pick it up. Check to see if your fishmonger has removed the small pin bones in the middle of the fish, above the belly. If not, remove them yourself with a pair of tweezers. Paul usually trims the meat off the belly and the tail of the salmon (and freezes it to use in a quiche) and just uses the thickest section. This ensures even cooking. Cut the side into six even slices.

Heat a heavy frying pan with the oil. Season the salmon slices with salt and pepper and place carefully in the pan. If the pan is not hot enough the slices will stick. Cook over a medium heat for 4 minutes without moving the slices, then turn them over and cook for another 3 minutes. They should be ready; you can take a peek inside by opening the flesh with a spatula or your fingers. If it is still a little pink, cook for another minute.

Serve on warm plates, with just about any vegetable accompaniment you like and a good ladleful of the sauce.

sautéed fillets of salmon with a champ sauce

This is not so much salmon with a sauce as salmon with some very creamy mash, or *pommes mousseline* as the French would call it. You may make the sauce (champ) as creamy as you prefer, or as firm as you prefer. And, of course, you may add chopped spring onions (scallions) if you want it to be proper champ.

Serves 8

8 skinless salmon fillets, weighing about 175 g (6 oz) each

2 tablespoons oil

Salt and freshly ground white pepper

A few salad leaves, to serve

3–4 tablespoons Vinaigrette Dressing (see page 85)

FOR THE CHAMP SAUCE

300 g (10 oz) potatoes, peeled and cut into generous 2.5 cm (1 in) cubes

½ small onion, chopped

175–200 ml (6–8 fl oz) whipping cream

Salt and freshly ground white pepper

4–6 tablespoons snipped fresh chives, plus extra to garnish

First make the champ sauce. Cover the potatoes and onion with cold salted water in a small saucepan, then bring to the boil over a medium heat and simmer until the potatoes are very soft. Drain off the liquid, add the cream to the potatoes and bring to the boil. Take off the heat and purée in a food processor. Season to taste and keep warm. If you prefer a more saucy consistency make the champ in the same way using just 200 g (8 oz) of potatoes.

Check that the salmon fillets are boneless. If there are any bones remaining, remove with a pair of tweezers.

Heat a large frying pan over a high heat, add the oil and tilt to coat the pan. Season the salmon fillets with salt and pepper. Fry them quickly for about 2 minutes on each side.

Add the chives to the potato purée, and spoon generously onto warm plates. Place a salmon fillet on the sauce, and top with a few salad leaves tossed in a little vinaigrette dressing and garnish with chives.

salmon fishcakes
with spring onions

These are not just any old fishcakes with way too much mash and not nearly enough fish. In fact, you'll find that there is no potato in this recipe at all. It is based on an American-style recipe which is full of large chunks of fish. Go ahead and try it with different fish, even mincing in crab or prawns.

Serves 4

500 g (1 lb 2 oz) boneless salmon
100 g (4 oz) spring onions, finely chopped
100 g (4 oz) Mayonnaise (see page 232)
100 g (4 oz) fresh breadcrumbs, soaked in milk and then squeezed
1 egg
1 tablespoon chopped fresh parsley
1 teaspoon fresh thyme leaves
Salt and cayenne pepper
A small salad, to serve
Mayonnaise, Hollandaise sauce, tomato chutney or yoghurt, to serve

FOR COATING AND COOKING
50 g (2 oz) ground almonds mixed with 50 g (2 oz) fresh breadcrumbs
3 tablespoons vegetable oil
3 tablespoons butter

To prepare the salmon, first make sure there are no bones. If there are, cut them away and discard these and any brown bits. Cut the salmon into thin strips, and then into 5 mm (¼ in) dice, and place in a bowl. Mince half the salmon to a rough purée in a food processor, then mix all the fish with the spring onions, mayonnaise, breadcrumbs, egg and herbs, and season with salt and cayenne pepper.

Divide the mixture into 12 portions and form each into a neat patty, about 8 cm (3¼ in) in diameter. Dredge each fishcake in the almond/breadcrumb mixture and pat to coat evenly with the crumbs.

To cook, heat half the oil in a heavy frying pan and add the butter. When the butter foams, add six of the fishcakes. Cook over a medium-high heat for about 3 minutes on each side. Transfer the cakes to kitchen paper while you cook the remaining six cakes.

Serve with a small salad and a favourite sauce, such as mayonnaise or Hollandaise, or tomato chutney or yoghurt.

fried trout in oatmeal with tomato and sorrel cream

Trout seems to have had its reputation spoilt recently by the poor-quality farmed product. However, a good wild fish is something to savour. Paul can still remember the sweetness and flavour of the trout fished from the River Bann that he ate almost 30 years ago. Sorrel, cream and trout are a magnificent combination; you really must try it.

Serves 4

8 small trout fillets, scaled but skin on
250 g (9 oz) rolled oats
Salt and freshly ground white pepper
3 tablespoons vegetable oil
2 tablespoons butter

FOR THE TOMATO AND SORREL CREAM
Butter
1 cup finely shredded sorrel leaves
1 large plum tomato, peeled, seeded and diced
Salt and freshly ground white pepper
200 ml (7 fl oz) double cream

To cook the trout, first make sure there are no bones. If there are, remove them with a pair of tweezers. Rinse the fillets and drain in a colander. Spread the oats on a large plate. Season the trout fillets lightly with salt and pepper, then roll them in the oats. Press the oats onto each fillet with your hands.

Heat a large frying pan over a moderate heat and add half the oil and half the butter. Wait until the butter is foaming, then add four fillets and fry for 2 minutes on each side. Transfer the fillets to a baking tray lined with kitchen paper and keep them warm in a low oven while you cook the remaining ones in the rest of the oil and butter.

To make the tomato and sorrel cream, melt the butter in a small saucepan over a gentle heat. As the butter is melting, add the sorrel, tomato and a little salt and pepper. Cook gently for about 2 minutes, then add the cream. Turn up the heat a little and bring the cream to the boil. Boil gently until the cream thickens to a sauce consistency, stirring occasionally. Remove from the heat, check the seasoning and adjust to taste.

To serve, lay two trout fillets on each warm plate and surround them with a few spoonfuls of the tomato and sorrel cream.

fillets of trout with tomato compote and chervil and olive oil dressing

Make this dish in late summer, when the wild trout is in season, tomatoes are at their best and chervil is young and fragrant.

Serves 4

4 trout fillets, weighing about 175 g (6 oz) each
150 ml (¼ pint) dry white wine
1 teaspoon light olive oil
1 teaspoon salt

FOR THE TOMATO COMPOTE
2 shallots, finely chopped
½ garlic clove, finely chopped
2 tablespoons light olive oil
1 teaspoon tomato purée
6 plum tomatoes, peeled, seeded, and coarsely chopped
Salt and freshly ground white pepper

FOR THE CHERVIL AND OLIVE OIL DRESSING
1 small bunch of fresh chervil
¼ teaspoon salt
Freshly ground white pepper
Juice of 1 lemon
150 ml (¼ pint) extra-virgin olive oil

First make the tomato compote. Sweat the shallots and garlic in the oil for about 2 minutes over a medium heat, then add the tomato purée, tomatoes and a little salt and pepper. Bring to the boil quickly, simmer for 2 minutes and then remove from the heat.

To make the chervil and olive oil dressing, pick the chervil leaves off their stalks (reserve the stalks) and coarsely chop the leaves. In a small bowl, mix the salt and pepper with the lemon juice and then stir in the oil. Finally, stir in the chopped chervil leaves. Set aside.

To cook the trout, carefully trim the fillets. Scale them with a dull serrated knife and take out any small bones with a pair of tweezers. Rinse the fillets in cold water and drain in a colander.

Place the wine in a wide saucepan with the chervil stalks, oil and salt and bring to the boil. Carefully put the trout fillets into the wine, cover and simmer very gently for 2 minutes. Remove from the heat and allow to stand for 1 minute before serving.

Spoon the tomato compote onto four warm plates and drizzle each plate with the chervil olive oil dressing. Quickly place a trout fillet on each plate and serve immediately.

gratin of trout with cucumber ribbons and dill

This gratin technique uses a cream sauce and can be applied to any meat or fish dish. It just adds another dimension. However, if you don't have a grill, this dish will taste fine without grilling it.

Serves 4

4 trout fillets, weighing about 200 g (8 oz) each
Salt and freshly ground white pepper
1 cucumber
2 tablespoons unsalted butter

FOR THE CREAM SAUCE
4 shallots, finely sliced
250 ml (9 fl oz) dry white wine, preferably Riesling
250 ml (9 fl oz) double cream
1 tablespoon Dijon mustard
1 small bunch of fresh dill, picked and chopped
100 ml (3½ fl oz) whipping cream, whipped to soft peaks

Preheat the grill to its highest setting.

First make the cream sauce. Combine the shallots and wine in a small saucepan and boil over a moderately high heat until you have about 6 tablespoons of liquid left. Add the cream and boil gently until it thickens to a sauce consistency. Strain through a fine mesh sieve into a clean saucepan, and reserve in a warm place while you prepare the trout.

To prepare the trout, trim and scale the trout fillets. Check that all the bones have been removed and take out any that remain with a pair of tweezers. Rinse the fillets in cold water and drain in a colander. Cut each fillet into six diamond-shaped pieces (simply cut the fillet across following the angle at the top of the fillet). Season these pieces with salt and pepper and arrange in a steaming basket. Steam for 2 minutes.

While the fish is steaming, prepare the cucumber ribbons. Peel the cucumber and discard the skin. Now, using the peeler, take long ribbon-like strips off the cucumber until you reach the seeds. Continue round the cucumber like this until you have made ribbons of the whole cucumber

Melt the butter in a saucepan with 4 tablespoons of water. Add the cucumber ribbons and some salt and pepper and cook over a high heat for about 2 minutes, or until the ribbons are cooked but still remain slightly crunchy.

To serve, bring the sauce back to the boil then remove it from the heat. Whisk in the mustard and chopped dill.

Divide the cucumber ribbons between four warm heatproof plates and spread them out to form beds for the trout. Arrange the fillets on top of the cucumber, alternating skin-side up and skin-side down to form a mosaic-like pattern.

Fold the whipped cream into the sauce and spoon a generous amount over each fillet. Place each plate under the grill until the sauce browns beautifully (about 1 minute). Serve at once.

cod fish pie with mustard sauce

This recipe is Paul's own version of one of his all-time favourite dishes, which he still makes whenever he has a craving for comfort food. We're sure you'll agree it's the perfect remedy for your own cravings.

Serves 4

50 g (2 oz) unsalted butter

2 leeks, washed, trimmed and finely sliced

140 g (5 oz) button mushrooms, sliced

2 large potatoes, thinly sliced

Salt and freshly ground black pepper

8 eggs

300 ml (1/2 pint) milk

6 tablespoons chopped fresh dill

600 g (1 lb 5 oz) skinless, boneless smoked cod fillet, cut into 4 cm (1 1/2 in) pieces

100 g (4 oz) Cheddar cheese, grated

Fresh dill sprigs, to garnish

FOR THE MUSTARD SAUCE

250 ml (9 fl oz) double cream

3–4 tablespoons wholegrain mustard

Salt and freshly ground black pepper

Preheat the oven to 220°C/425°C/Gas 7. Take a rectangular microwave and ovenproof dish, 5 cm (2 in) deep. Place the butter, leeks and mushrooms in the dish, and then add the potatoes in an even layer. Season generously and add a splash of water. Cover with non-PVC plastic film, and pierce a couple of times with a knife. Microwave on full power for 5 minutes, or until the potatoes are done.

If you don't have a microwave, melt the butter in a large saucepan. Add the leeks and sauté until softened, then add the mushrooms and cook for a further minute. Transfer to an ovenproof dish. Cook the potatoes in a saucepan of boiling, salted water for 8–10 minutes or until just tender, then drain and layer over the leeks and mushrooms.

Place the eggs and milk in a jug and beat until combined. Add 3–4 tablespoons of the dill and season generously with salt and pepper. Scatter the fish on top of the potatoes, season with salt, and pour over the egg mixture, stirring slightly. Place in the oven for 10 minutes.

Remove from the oven, sprinkle with the Cheddar cheese and then return to the oven for about 5 minutes. To finish, preheat the grill to hot and place the dish underneath until the cheese is bubbling and golden.

To make the mustard sauce, reduce the cream in a saucepan until slightly thickened, then remove from the heat. Stir in the mustard and the remaining dill, and season.

Divide the pie between four warm plates and spoon the sauce over. Garnish with sprigs of dill.

fillets of cod with a smoky garlic and parsley butter

The smokiness in this dish comes from the very smoky outside trimmings of a whole side of smoked salmon. If you can't find these, use trimmings from smoked cod or haddock; or even smoked ham trimmings would work well. The final alternative would be to use 'smoked garlic' itself, which you can find in many supermarkets nowadays. Use the skin to help give extra smokiness.

Serves 4

4 portions of thick, boneless, skinless cod fillets, weighing about 200 g (8 oz) each

100 g (4 oz) plain white flour, for dredging

2 tablespoons vegetable oil

A knob of butter

Salt and freshly ground white pepper

FOR THE PARSLEY BUTTER

140 g (5 oz) unsalted butter

50 g (2 oz) smoked salmon trimmings

3 garlic cloves, crushed

1 small bunch of fresh parsley

3 tablespoons lemon juice

Salt and freshly ground black pepper

FOR THE VEGETABLES

140 g (5 oz) carrots, diced

140 g (5 oz) leeks, washed, trimmed and diced

140 g (5 oz) potatoes, peeled and diced

First make the parsley butter. Melt the butter in a small saucepan, with the smoked salmon trimming and the crushed garlic. Heat gently for about 10 minutes or until the butter has clarified. Strain the butter through a sieve and return it to the pan. Then allow the butter to rest off the heat for 30 minutes, to let the flavours infuse.

Meanwhile, pick the parsley leaves off their stalks and blanch them in boiling water for 1 minute. Refresh under very cold water, then drain, pat dry with kitchen paper and chop roughly. Set aside.

Strain the clarified butter through a fine sieve and add the lemon juice, and the salt and pepper.

Blanch or steam the vegetables until they are tender, then refresh them under cold water and reserve.

To cook the cod fillets, season them with some salt and pepper and dredge them in the flour. In a large frying pan, heat the vegetable oil until almost smoking, then add the knob of butter and the cod fillets. Cook the fillets over a medium heat for about 4 minutes on each side. Be careful not to treat them roughly, or they will tend to break up.

To serve, warm the vegetables and parsley leaves in the clarified butter. Divide this mixture between warm plates and add a cod fillet to each serving.

freshly pickled cod with a parsley aïoli

Poached fish served with a minimum of fuss is pure and delicious. Here the cod is poached and allowed to cool in an aromatic broth called a *court bouillon*. It can be served straight away, or chilled for a day or two and allowed to return to room temperature before serving. Add as much or as little garlic to the aïoli as you prefer.

Serves 6

6 cod steaks, weighing about 100g (4 oz) each, lightly salted and left overnight

FOR THE COURT BOUILLON

50 ml (2 fl oz) white wine vinegar

250 ml (9 fl oz) dry white wine

1 small carrot, neatly sliced

1 small onion, neatly sliced

1 garlic clove, sliced

1 bay leaf

½ teaspoon coriander seeds

½ teaspoon fennel seeds

6 white peppercorns

1 tablespoon salt

FOR THE AÏOLI

1 small bunch of fresh parsley, stalks removed

3 egg yolks

2–4 garlic cloves, finely chopped

1½ tablespoons lemon juice

½ teaspoon salt

250 ml (9 fl oz) light olive oil

250 ml (9 fl oz) vegetable oil

First make the *court bouillon*. Put all the ingredients in a large saucepan with 500 ml (18 fl oz) of water. Bring to the boil over a medium heat and simmer gently for 15–20 minutes, or until the carrots are tender. Remove from the heat and allow to infuse for at least 1 hour.

To cook the cod, return the *court bouillon* to the boil. Add the cod steaks and simmer over a very low heat for about 2 minutes. Remove the pan from the heat and allow the cod to finish cooking as it cools down.

To make the aïoli, bring a saucepan of water to the boil, add the parsley leaves and blanch for 30 seconds; then drain and refresh under cold water. Pat dry with kitchen paper and chop roughly.

In a food processor, combine the parsley, egg yolks, garlic, lemon juice and salt. Blend for a few seconds, then slowly add the oils in a steady stream until emulsified. Set aside.

To serve, place the cod steaks on a large serving platter with some vegetables from the *court bouillon* and drizzle over a little of the liquid. Serve the aïoli on the side.

crisp fried cod with lentils and vinegar

This recipe takes its inspiration from deep-fried cod and mushy peas. This version is very much lighter and prettier yet has the same appealing textures.

Serves 4

Vegetable oil, for deep-frying
8 tablespoons whipping cream
2 egg whites
4 boneless cod fillets, weighing about 100 g (4 oz) each
2 teaspoons chopped fresh parsley, to garnish

FOR THE LENTILS

100 g (4 oz) Puy lentils
700 ml (1¼ pints) chicken or vegetable stock or water
1 teaspoon salt
2 tablespoons finely diced onion
2 tablespoons finely diced carrot
2 tablespoons finely diced leek
2 tablespoons finely diced celery
2 tablespoons finely diced potato
6 tablespoons sherry vinegar
100 g (4 oz) unsalted butter, chilled and diced

FOR THE SPICED FLOUR

8 tablespoons plain white flour
4 teaspoons baking powder
1 teaspoon cayenne pepper
1 teaspoon ground thyme
1 teaspoon white pepper
1 teaspoon garlic pepper
1 teaspoon salt

First cook the lentils. Rinse them in plenty of cold water, then put them into a small pan with the stock or water and the salt. Bring to the boil and simmer for 10 minutes. Add the diced vegetable and cook for a further 10–15 minutes, or until everything is fully cooked. Add the vinegar and whisk in the diced butter. Keep warm. If you need to plan ahead, the lentils can be kept for a day or two in the fridge. If you are doing this, do not add the butter until you reheat the lentils just before serving.

Heat the oil in a deep-fat fryer to 190°C/375°F.

Sift the ingredients for the spiced flour together. In a small bowl, mix the cream with the egg whites. Dredge the cod fillets in the spiced flour. 'Massage' the fish in the cream mixture, then dredge them in the flour again. Repeat if you prefer a slightly thicker crust.

Carefully drop two of the cod fillets into the hot oil and cook for about 4 minutes, until they are crisp and golden. Drain on kitchen paper. Keep warm while you cook the remaining fillets.

To serve, spoon generous amounts of lentils onto warm serving plates and top each serving with a cod fillet. Finish with a sprinkling of parsley.

grilled black sole
with a herb butter

Black sole is what we call Dover sole in Ireland because it has a blacker skin than the much-loved lemon sole. This is not a new recipe, or an innovative one, but it is one of our most favourite things to eat in the whole world.

Serves 4

4 Dover sole, weighing about
450 g (1 lb) each
2 tablespoons vegetable oil
Salt and freshly ground white pepper
Chips or boiled potatoes, to serve
2 lemons, halved, to garnish
Fresh herb sprigs, to garnish

FOR THE HERB BUTTER
125 ml (4 fl oz) dry white wine
2 shallots, sliced
200 g (8 oz) butter, softened
2 anchovy fillets, roughly chopped
1 tablespoon Dijon mustard
1 tablespoon Worcestershire sauce,
(optional)
1 tablespoon each chopped fresh chives,
parsley, tarragon and chervil

Preheat the grill or barbecue to high.

First, make the herb butter. Boil the wine with the shallots until the wine has almost evaporated. Place the butter in a food processor and add the anchovy fillets, mustard, Worcestershire sauce, if using, herbs, and salt and pepper and the wine reduction with the shallots. Blend quickly until smooth. Taste for seasoning, adding more salt or mustard as you prefer. With a spatula, scoop the butter onto a large piece of clingfilm. Roll the butter into a cylinder shape and refrigerate until ready to use.

Prepare the sole by removing the black skin and scaling the white side or, if you prefer, you can ask your fishmonger to do this for you. Rinse the sole and drain in a colander. Trim off the fins with a pair of scissors, cut off and discard the head. Season the fish with salt and pepper and rub with a little oil. Grill for about 5 minutes on each side. (If you are using a barbecue, remember to clean and oil it well to prevent the fish flesh from sticking.)

To serve, place each sole on a warm plate with a good tablespoon of the herb butter right on top. Garnish with a lemon half and a sprig of chervil. Serve with chips or steamed new potatoes.

roast fillets of brill with potato scales and warm leek vinaigrette

When we first started cooking fish with potato scales it seemed hilarious and very Irish indeed. In fact the technique comes from France where they do it with potato julienne, grated potato, potato ribbons, etc. The point is that the potato gives the dish a beautiful contrast of textures and keeps the fish moist as it cooks – those clever French.

Serves 6

6–8 baby potatoes, scrubbed
Salt and freshly ground white pepper
200 g (8 oz) unsalted butter, melted
6 thick brill fillets, weighing about 140 g (5 oz) each
Plain white flour, for dredging
1½ tablespoons vegetable oil

FOR THE WARM LEEK VINAIGRETTE
3 tablespoons butter
450 g (1 lb) leeks, washed, trimmed and finely sliced
Salt and freshly ground white pepper
6 plum tomatoes, peeled, seeded and diced
4½ tablespoons white wine vinegar
2 teaspoons wholegrain mustard
200 ml (8 fl oz) light olive oil

Slice the potatoes as thinly as possible (about 3 mm/⅛ in), using a sharp knife or a vegetable slicer. Season them lightly with salt, cover with a damp cloth and allow to stand for 5 minutes. After this time you will notice that the potatoes have given off plenty of water and are limp and pliable. Pat the slices dry and then pour over them about 140 g (5 oz) of the melted butter, stirring to coat the potatoes in the butter.

Season the brill fillets with salt and pepper, dredge lightly in flour and place on a plate. Arrange the potato slices on one side of the brill, overlapping the slices slightly to give the effect of fish scales. When all the fillets are covered, chill them for at least 30 minutes to allow the potato scales to stick firmly.

Preheat the oven to 180°C/350°F/Gas 4. To cook the fish, heat a large, heavy-based ovenproof frying pan over a moderate heat. Add the oil and remaining butter and heat until the butter is foaming. Carefully place the fillets in the pan, potato-side down, and cook for about 3 minutes until the potatoes are beginning to brown nicely. Turn the fillets over and cook for about 30 seconds to seal the other side, then turn the fish again and place the pan in the oven for 5 minutes, or until the fillets are cooked and firm to the touch.

To make the warm leek vinaigrette, melt the butter with 200 ml (7 fl oz) of water over a high heat in a large saucepan. Add the leeks and a little salt and cook for about 5 minutes, stirring frequently. Add the tomatoes and a few twists of pepper and remove from the heat. In a small bowl, whisk together the vinegar, mustard, ¼ teaspoon of salt and some more freshly ground white pepper. Whisk in the oil and then check and adjust the seasoning to taste. Add the leek mixture.

To serve, carefully turn the fillets onto warm plates and surround each one with the warm leek vinaigrette.

smoked haddock hash with poached eggs and mustard mayonnaise

This recipe is the perfect dish to choose for either a lazy Sunday brunch or a light lunch. You could think of it as a potential alternative to eggs Benedict. For a bit of variation we'd recommend that you give it a go serving it with a Hollandaise sauce instead of the mayo… it's really wonderful!

Serves 6–8

750 g (1 lb 10 oz) smoked haddock

3 tablespoons white wine vinegar

Salt

25 g (1 oz) salt

25 g (1 oz) butter, plus extra for dotting the hash

1 small red onion, sliced

½ yellow pepper, diced

½ red pepper, diced

4 spring onions, finely sliced

500 g (1 lb 2 oz) potatoes, peeled and cut into 2 cm (¾ in) dice

2 tablespoons light olive oil

2 tablespoons chopped fresh parsley

1 tablespoon snipped fresh chives, (optional)

2–4 tablespoons wholegrain mustard

200 g (8 oz) Mayonnaise (see page 232)

6–8 eggs, to serve

Fresh parsley sprigs, to garnish

Trim and bone the haddock. Bring 2 litres (3½ pints) of water to the boil and add the vinegar and 1 tablespoon salt. Reduce to a simmer, add the haddock and poach gently for 8–10 minutes. Remove the haddock from the water and drain in a colander. When it is cool enough to handle, flake into 2 cm (¾ in) chunks.

Melt the butter in a large saucepan, with 4 tablespoons of water. Add the red onion, peppers, spring onions and a little salt. Cook over a moderate heat for about 5 minutes, until all the liquid has evaporated and the vegetables are just starting to brown. Set aside.

In a large frying pan, fry the potatoes in the oil until golden brown in colour. Now add the haddock and the vegetables. Mix together gently and then press down evenly with a spatula. Dot the hash with a few pieces of butter, cover and cook gently for 5–7 minutes. Alternatively, the hash can be attractively presented as individual portions simply by using pastry rings or individual small frying pans. Reduce the cooking time slightly, using the colour of the potatoes as a guide.

Mix the mustard and mayonnaise together.

Lightly poach the eggs in a wide pan of simmering water (see page 84).

To serve, turn the hash out onto a large warm serving plate or simply spoon onto individual plates. Serve with the poached eggs and mustard mayonnaise. Garnish with sprigs of parsley.

trio of seafood with a brown butter vinaigrette

This is another of our restaurant dishes. Our customers love the idea of tasting three different types of fish in one dish. That does, of course, make it more difficult to serve – so feel free to stick to just one variety. The thing we love about this dish is the vinaigrette, with its toasty hazelnut flavours.

Serves 4

225 g (8 oz) turbot fillet
225 g (8 oz) hake fillet
225 g (8 oz) salmon fillet
Oil, for deep frying
8 waxy potatoes, preferably Roseval
Salt and freshly ground white pepper
2 large carrots, cut in julienne strips
50 g (2 oz) plain white flour
2 tablespoons butter
175 g (6 oz) buttered, cooked spinach

FOR THE BROWN BUTTER VINAIGRETTE
125 g (4½ oz) unsalted butter
1 tablespoon wholegrain mustard
2 tablespoons Forum red wine vinegar or
1 tablespoon ordinary red wine vinegar
and 1 tablespoon balsamic vinegar
Salt and freshly ground white pepper

Trim the fish fillets neatly and remove any remaining bones with a pair of tweezers. Carefully cut each fillet into four pieces. Before cooking the fish, prepare the brown butter vinaigrette and the vegetables.

To make the vinaigrette, heat the butter in a saucepan until it turns a deep golden brown (*beurre noisette*). Now, quickly strain it through a very fine sieve to remove all the milk solids. Whisk the mustard into the vinegars and then whisk in the warm butter (it should be neither too hot nor too cold if it is to emulsify). Add a little salt and pepper to taste.

Preheat the oil to 160°C/320°F in a deep-fat fryer.

Cook the potatoes in their skins in boiling, salted water. Allow to cool and then peel them and slice into neat coins. Place in a ceramic dish, season with salt and pepper and cover with clingfilm. Reheat in the microwave, on full power, for 90 seconds just before serving.

Dust the carrot julienne lightly in the flour. Deep-fry until the strips stop sizzling. Immediately drain on kitchen paper and season lightly with salt. These crispy carrot strips can be prepared well ahead and then reheated in a low oven.

To cook the fish, season it with salt and pepper. Heat a large frying pan, (preferably non-stick) over a moderately high heat. Add the butter and let it sizzle. Now add the fish pieces. Cook for about 3 minutes on each side. When the fish is cooked, remove it to a warm plate and cover while you present the vegetables.

Start by laying three small piles of the cooked and buttered spinach on each warm plate. Place a few slices of potatoes between each pile of spinach and a small tower of carrots in the centre. Place the fish on the spinach piles and spoon the brown butter vinaigrette around and over the various items on the plate. Serve immediately.

seviche with tomato lime and fresh coriander

Although this recipe does not sound the slightest bit Irish, it actually is. This is because the most important element in a seviche is the freshness and quality of the fish. And here in Ireland, we have the best. You could use salmon, hake, brill, scallops, mackerel or even halibut, to name just a few, for this recipe.

Serves 4

140 g (5 oz) very fresh hake, skinned
140 g (5 oz) very fresh salmon, skinned
150 ml (¼ pint) fresh lime juice
1 teaspoon salt
Freshly ground black pepper
2 ripe tomatoes, peeled, seeded and diced
2 tablespoons thinly sliced red onion
2–4 fresh chillies, seeded and thinly sliced
1 small avocado, peeled, stoned and diced
3 tablespoons chopped fresh coriander
2 tablespoons olive oil
Finely sliced lettuce, to serve
Fresh coriander sprigs, to garnish

Check the fish for bones and remove any remaining bones with a pair of tweezers. Cut into fine slices or into 1 cm (½ in) dice. In a ceramic or stainless steel bowl, combine the fish with the lime juice, salt and pepper. Cover and chill for 2 hours, stirring occasionally.

Remove from the fridge and add the tomatoes, onion, chillies, avocado, coriander and oil. Allow to marinate for 30 minutes more.

Taste for seasoning, adding more salt and chilli, if preferred. Serve on a 'nest' of sliced lettuce and garnish each serving with a sprig of fresh coriander.

risotto cakes with sautéed prawns and a fresh tomato and basil sauce

Risotto cakes are one of those items that are hard to pass by on a restaurant menu, in Jeanne's mind, anyway. Being so easy to prepare, they are worth trying, especially if you have leftover risotto in the fridge.

Serves 4

16–20 cooked prawn tails
2 tablespoons vegetable oil
2 tablespoons butter

FOR THE RISOTTO CAKES
50 g (2 oz) butter
1 shallot, finely chopped
140 g (5 oz) arborio rice
600 ml (1 pint) fish stock
Salt and freshly ground white pepper
2 tablespoons chopped fresh parsley, plus extra to garnish
2 tablespoons chopped fresh basil, plus extra to garnish
50 g (2 oz) plain white flour

FOR THE TOMATO AND BASIL SAUCE
1 shallot, finely chopped
1 small red chilli, seeded and finely chopped
2 garlic cloves, finely chopped
2 tablespoons vegetable oil
2 teaspoons tomato purée
2 teaspoons finely chopped anchovy fillet
1 kg (2 lb 4 oz) tomatoes, peeled and roughly chopped
3 tablespoons extra-virgin olive oil
3 tablespoons chopped fresh basil

First make the risotto cakes. Melt half the butter in a heavy-based frying pan and fry the shallot gently until soft and transparent. Add the rice and stir well so that all the grains get coated with the butter. After 2 minutes, slowly start adding the fish stock, a ladle at a time, until the rice is tender and the stock has been absorbed. Season to taste, and add the herbs. Turn the risotto out onto a baking sheet to let it cool down.

Once it is cool, take a small handful, roll it into a ball and coat it lightly with the flour. Flatten into a little cake, about 1 cm (½ in) thick and 3–4 cm (1¼–1½ in) wide. Make two for each person. To cook the cakes, heat a heavy-based frying pan over a medium-high heat and add the remaining butter. Fry the cakes until nice and golden brown and crisp. This may need to be done in batches; if so, the first can be kept warm in a low oven (110°C/225°F/Gas ¼).

To make the tomato and basil sauce, sweat the shallot, chilli and garlic in the vegetable oil. When soft, add the tomato purée and then the anchovy. Add the tomatoes and leave to simmer for 5–8 minutes, just until the tomatoes have collapsed and everything is heated through. Just before serving, add the olive oil and basil.

To cook the prawn tails, take them out of their shells. Heat a heavy-based frying pan over a high heat. Add the oil and butter, and sauté the prawn tails until lightly browned and heated through. This should only take a couple of minutes.

To assemble the dish, place two risotto cakes in the centre of each warm plate and top with a spoonful of the chunky tomato basil sauce. Arrange the prawn tails on top of the sauce and around the cakes, then ladle some more sauce around the plate. Garnish with herbs and serve at once.

spaghettini molly malone

Wonderful cockles and mussels thrive all around the coast of Ireland. They often suit a good splash of cream or a few knobs of butter, but for Paul this treatment with white wine, garlic, and olive oil is his favourite. We heard once that it's a recipe Molly brought back after having a fling with Marco Polo on her holidays.

Serves 4

1 large red chilli, seeded and
finely chopped

4 garlic cloves, chopped

8 tablespoons extra-virgin olive oil

1 kg (2 lb 4 oz) cockles

1 kg (2 lb 4 oz) mussels

250 ml (9 fl oz) dry white wine

3 tablespoons onion, finely chopped

2 fresh parsley stalks

450 g (1 lb) packet of spaghettini

2 tablespoons roughly chopped
fresh parsley

Place the chilli (reserving a little to garnish), garlic and oil in a small bowl, and cook in the microwave on full power for 1 minute. Alternatively, warm over a gentle heat in a small saucepan for about 5 minutes. Set aside.

Wash and scrub the cockles and mussels carefully, scraping off the beards from the mussels. Rinse in plenty of clean water, and discard any mussels that are open or do not close when tapped with a knife.

Bring the wine, onion and parsley stalks to the boil in a large saucepan over a high heat. Add the cockles and mussels, cover and boil vigorously for 3–4 minutes, or until all the cockles and mussels have opened. Discard any mussels that remain closed. Drain into a colander with a bowl underneath to catch all that precious cooking liquid. Reserve the broth and, as soon as they are cool enough, remove about two-thirds of the cockles and mussels from their shells. Place both the shelled cockles and mussels and the ones in their shells in a saucepan and pour the reserved broth over them, leaving behind the last few spoonfuls of liquid as it will be quite gritty.

Cook the spaghettini in plenty of boiling, salted water according to the packet instructions.

Meanwhile, heat the cockles and mussels in the broth, adding the chilli and garlic oil to the pan. Add the herbs, reserving some of the chopped parsley to garnish. Do not allow to boil or continue to cook as the cockles and mussels will toughen.

Drain the spaghettini, toss the pasta with the cockles and mussels mixture, sprinkle over the reserved chilli and parsley, and serve at once in warm bowls.

king prawn kebabs with a sun-dried tomato vinaigrette

When we first cooked this recipe nearly 15 years ago in California it was very mod and cutting edge. Nowadays it's almost old-fashioned. To us, whether it's new or old doesn't really matter. Does it work? Yes, it's delicious!

Serves 6

36 large raw prawns, weighing about 900 g (2 lb), peeled and their intestinal tracts removed

12 spring onions

$\frac{1}{2}$ teaspoon salt

$\frac{1}{4}$ teaspoon freshly ground black pepper

1 tablespoon chopped fresh parsley

1 tablespoon light olive oil

Mixed salad leaves, to serve

Fresh parsley sprigs, to garnish

FOR THE SUN-DRIED TOMATO VINAIGRETTE

12 sun-dried tomatoes in oil, weighing about 100 g (4 oz), roughly chopped

200 ml (7 fl oz) light olive oil

1 teaspoon lemon juice

Salt and freshly ground black pepper

$\frac{1}{2}$ teaspoon chilli powder (optional)

Soak six wooden skewers in water for at least 30 minutes. Light the barbecue.

First make the sun-dried tomato vinaigrette. Blend together all the ingredients in a food processor for about a minute or until the vinaigrette has a fairly smooth texture. Taste for seasoning because sun-dried tomatoes vary greatly in the amount of salt and flavour they contain. Adjust the salt and pepper to taste.

In a large bowl, toss the prawns and spring onions with the seasonings, parsley and oil. Thread six prawns and two onions onto each skewer, starting and finishing with an onion.

Grill on the barbecue for 2 minutes on each side. Serve on warm plates, with a generous spoonful of the sun-dried tomato vinaigrette and a few salad leaves and sprigs of parsley.

If you want to try this dish, but don't feel like having a barbecue, cooking the kebabs under a conventional grill, on a high heat for 3–4 minutes on each side, or in a frying pan, for 2 minutes on each side, will also work well.

steamed symphony of seafood with a saffron butter vinaigrette

Steaming is a great and very forgiving technique for cooking complex dishes like this one. A selection of six to eight kinds of very fresh fish and shellfish is needed; use what is available – the following are just suggestions. Serve with boiled potatoes.

Serves 4

About 125 g (4½ oz) each of 6–8 of the following: salmon, brill, lemon sole, hake, monkfish, haddock fillets, prawns mussels, scallops
Butter, for steaming

FOR THE SAFFRON BUTTER VINAIGRETTE
140 g (5 oz) unsalted butter
150 ml (¼ pint) dry white wine
1 shallot, finely chopped
A pinch of saffron strands
150 ml (¼ pint) fish stock
Salt and freshly ground white pepper
2 tomatoes, peeled, seeded and chopped
2 fresh tarragon sprigs, chopped
Buttered cooked spinach, to serve

Carefully trim the fish fillets, making sure that they are nicely shaped and free of bones. Remove any remaining bones with a pair of tweezers. Cut all of the seafood into appropriate sizes, making sure you have four pieces of each type you are using. Save any trimmings and bones to infuse the vinaigrette.

To make the saffron butter vinaigrette, first clarify the butter by bringing it to a simmer in a small saucepan. Skim off any froth that comes to the surface. When the surface has cleared, let the milky solids settle, and simply pour the butter off, leaving behind any watery, milky liquid. Discard the milky liquid and reserve the clarified butter.

Bring the wine to a simmer in a small saucepan, with the shallot, saffron strands and fish trimmings, until the liquid has reduced to about 3 tablespoons. Add the fish stock and simmer again – you should have about 200 ml (7 fl oz) of liquid left. Strain this liquid through a fine sieve. Season with salt and pepper. Add the tomatoes, tarragon and clarified butter and the vinaigrette is ready.

To steam the fish, butter a large steaming basket and arrange the pieces of fish carefully in it. Season with salt only (pepper at this stage makes the fish look dirty). Place over a saucepan of boiling water, cover and steam for about 4 minutes, until the fish is cooked.

To serve, divide the spinach between four warm plates. Arrange the fish nicely on top of the spinach, and spoon over the warm saffron butter vinaigrette.

meat, poultry and game

The meats in this chapter read like a veritable who's who from the fields and farmyards of Ireland. We've deliberately included recipes that use a good selection of meats, and different cuts, in order to give you as many cooking techniques as possible.

For example, with chicken you can cook escalopes with cream, drumsticks with garlic, stuffed breasts for an elegant meal or simply roast a whole bird, like our Roast Poussins with a Herb Bread Sauce (see page 121). Some of these techniques are tried and trusted favourites of ours. The method for cooking beef in the Warm Steak Salad with Anchovy and Caper Vinaigrette (see page 133) is Paul's favourite way, bar none, of cooking steaks. The steak is cut thick, grilled over a high heat and then sliced against the grain.

Of course, the quality of the product is paramount with main course meats and a good butcher will be your greatest ally here. It goes without saying that the meat should come from healthy, well-fed animals of the correct breed, and in Ireland good butchers are invaluable. They often know the farmers personally, and even the fields where the animals are reared. One of the most important aspects of good meat is how it is handled once the animal has been slaughtered. This is where a good butcher really comes into his own. The single most important factor in obtaining tender, flavourful meat is the ageing or hanging process. You may sometimes have wondered why you ended up with a tough or stringy piece of meat. Sometimes this is just down to the cut and its inherent character but, more often than not, the ageing process has been overlooked or ignored. This is because ageing is an expensive and time-consuming process. But surely most of us are willing to pay a little more for meat that is flavourful and tender?

One cooking detail that applies to virtually all the recipes in this chapter is 'resting' the meat. As meat (particularly the larger cuts) cooks the heat drives the moisture towards the centre and the fibres of the meat become quite tense. A resting period at the end of cooking allows the moisture and juices to redistribute themselves and the muscle structure to relax, which gives a more evenly cooked, juicier and softer piece of meat. The larger the cut, the longer the recommended resting period. The meat may lose some temperature, but remember you can always flash it in a hot oven or under the grill to bring it back to piping hot.

breasts of chicken stuffed with lobster and basil

This is a dish we do at our restaurant from time to time and customers just love it. It is a slightly showy dish that would suit an important dinner party. Practice it first, as there is quite a lot going on, but once you have the hang of it you will find it rather easy.

Serves 4

2 live lobsters, weighing about 450 g (1 lb) each

4 large skinless, boneless chicken breasts, weighing about 200 g (8 oz) each

200 ml (7 fl oz) single cream, chilled

2 tablespoons chopped fresh basil

2 tablespoons snipped fresh chives

Salt and freshly ground black pepper

2 tablespoons vegetable oil

Buttered noodles, to serve

A cooked green vegetable, such as chard, spinach or mange tout, to serve

FOR THE SAUCE

Lobster shell, from the body

2 tablespoons olive oil

4 shallots, thinly sliced

4 garlic cloves, crushed

2 tablespoons tomato purée

4 tablespoons port

4 tablespoons brandy

600 ml (1 pint) double cream

2 tablespoons chopped fresh basil

Preheat the oven to 200°C/400°F/Gas 6.

To cook the lobsters, bring a large saucepan of water to a vigorous boil. Put in the lobsters, cover and cook for about 12 minutes. Remove the lobsters from the saucepan and stop the cooking process by plunging them into a sink of cold water.

Insert a knife where the tail and body join and cut towards the tail, then remove the intestinal tract; the tail meat will now easily pull away from the shell. Break off the claws and crack the shells with a heavy knife. Remove the meat and any pieces of shell, reserving the body shell for the sauce. Cut the meat into 1 cm (½ in) dice.

To make the lobster and basil stuffing, remove all of the small 'fillets' attached to the underside of the chicken breasts. With a sharp knife remove any sinew from inside the fillets, then roughly mash the flesh with a heavy knife or in a food processor. Place the mashed chicken in a bowl and add the diced lobster, cream, basil, chives and salt and pepper. Beat this mixture vigorously with a wooden spoon until it comes together and looks sticky.

To prepare the breasts for stuffing, lay each one flat on a cutting board and make a long horizontal incision almost completely through it, so that you can open it out like a book. Season each breast and spoon the stuffing along the middle line. Fold both sides on top of the stuffing, moulding the breast into a good shape with your hands. Butter four sheets of foil about 25 cm (10 in) square and wrap each breast tightly, twisting the ends of the foil to help the breast keep its shape.

Heat a frying pan over a high heat, add the vegetable oil and seal the foil-wrapped breasts for about 4 minutes, turning them now and then. Place them in the oven for about 15 minutes, then remove them and allow to rest in a warm place.

While the breasts are in the oven, make the sauce. First, crush the lobster shells with a heavy cleaver or a clean, household hammer. Fry the shells in a pan with the olive oil over a high heat for 2 minutes. Add the shallots and garlic and fry for 2 more minutes. Add the tomato purée, port, brandy and 125 ml (4 fl oz) of water and boil until reduced by half. Add the cream and continue to boil until the sauce thickens. Strain the sauce through a fine sieve into a clean bowl and add the basil.

To serve, carefully unwrap the chicken breasts, allowing any juices to fall into the sauce. Slice each breast and arrange the slices attractively on warm plates. Spoon the sauce generously around. Serve with buttered noodles and a green vegetable.

roast chicken drumsticks with parsley and garlic

Drumsticks are a great snack food. They have a delicious rich texture that doesn't dry out on reheating. They are cheap and easy to buy, and kids like them too. Paul is a big fan, especially of this recipe which reminds him of his first trip to France because of the parsley and garlic, or *persillade* as the French call it.

Serves 4

12–16 chicken drumsticks
1 tablespoon olive oil
4 tablespoons butter
3 garlic cloves, finely chopped
2 tablespoons chopped fresh parsley
1 tablespoon lemon juice
Salt and freshly ground black pepper

Season the drumsticks generously with salt and pepper. Heat a large, heavy-based flameproof casserole over a moderate heat with the oil and half the butter. When the butter is foaming, add the drumsticks, and cook until lightly browned all over.

Cover and cook over a gentle heat for a further 25 minutes, making sure to turn the drumsticks frequently and constantly monitor the heat so that they fry gently.

Add the remaining butter, with the garlic, parsley and lemon juice, and allow to infuse away from the heat for a few minutes before serving.

sauté of chicken with tagliatelle, wild mushrooms and cream

This is such a great dish that we recommend you try it with rabbit, pork fillet, and even pheasant. It may not sound very Irish, but when you make it with your own hand-picked Irish porcini, no one will really care!

Serves 4

30 g (generous 1 oz) dried wild mushrooms, such as porcini or morels

4 skinless, boneless chicken breasts

Salt and freshly ground black pepper

5 tablespoons butter

2 shallots, finely chopped

100 ml (3½ fl oz) white wine

50 ml (2 fl oz) Madeira

150 ml (¼ pint) double cream

100 ml (3½ fl oz) chicken stock

TO SERVE

250 g (9 oz) tagliatelle, cooked according to packet instructions

½ Savoy cabbage, outer leaves removed, cored, shredded, sautéed and buttered

A few sautéed mushrooms

2 tablespoons snipped fresh chives, to garnish

Soak the mushrooms in warm water for 30 minutes. Drain and check that the stalks are free of dirt. Slice the larger mushrooms in half and leave the small ones whole.

Remove the small 'fillet' attached to the underside of each chicken breast. Place one breast firmly on a cutting board and slice at an angle into four escalopes. You now have five pieces from one breast. Repeat with the other breasts. Season with salt and pepper.

Heat 2 tablespoons of the butter in a large, heavy-based frying pan until it starts to foam. Add half the chicken pieces, in one layer. Cook slowly for 2 minutes on each side, then remove the pieces from the saucepan to a plate. Repeat with the remaining chicken pieces.

Melt the remaining butter in a medium saucepan over a medium heat and sauté the shallots. When they are soft and transparent, add the wine, Madeira and mushrooms. Cook slowly over a low heat until most of the liquid has evaporated. Add the cream, chicken stock and some salt and pepper and bring to a gentle boil. Reduce if necessary to achieve a nice sauce consistency (it should coat the back of a spoon).

Add the chicken pieces and let the sauce just come back to simmering point.

To serve, arrange a little pile of tagliatelle in the centre of each warm plate and put some of the cabbage beside it. Spoon five pieces of chicken and plenty of sauce over the pasta. Arrange the sautéed mushrooms around the plate and sprinkle with the chives. Serve immediately.

roast poussins with a herb bread sauce

Poussins differ from just any young chicken in that they have reached maturity and developed flavour, yet generally weigh only about 450 g (1 lb). We think they're great because everyone gets their own bird, with two legs and two breasts each. Poussins can be a bit tricky to eat, so serve with finger bowls and don't be afraid to use your fingers.

Serves 4

2 tablespoons light olive oil

2 tablespoons butter

8 garlic cloves, unpeeled and slightly crushed

4 fresh thyme sprigs

4 poussins, weighing about 450 g (1 lb) each, plus trimmings such as neck or wing tips (optional)

300 ml (½ pint) hot chicken stock

Seasonal vegetables, to serve

FOR THE HERB BREAD SAUCE

8 thick slices of white bread, crusts removed

450 ml (16 fl oz) milk

1 teaspoon fresh thyme leaves

4 tablespoons finely chopped fresh parsley

2 teaspoons finely chopped fresh rosemary

Preheat the oven to 200°C/400°F/Gas 6.

Heat the oil and 1 tablespoon of butter over a high heat in a roasting tin on the hob. Add the garlic, thyme and trimmings from the poussins, if using. Add the poussins and lightly brown them on all sides for about 5 minutes. Sit the browned poussins upright and roast for about 35–40 minutes, basting with the cooking juices occasionally.

Remove the poussins and keep them warm. Reserve the garlic and discard the thyme and trimmings. Skim off excess fat and deglaze the tin with the chicken stock, stirring well to scrape up all the caramelized juices off the bottom of the tin. Simmer for 2 minutes, then strain into a clean bowl. Whisk in the remaining tablespoon of butter and keep the gravy in a warm place.

To make the herb bread sauce, whizz the bread in a food processor to make breadcrumbs. Bring the milk to the boil in a saucepan and stir in the breadcrumbs. Squeeze the flesh from the reserved garlic cloves into the pan. Cook gently for 4–5 minutes, stirring, until thickened. Add the thyme, parsley and rosemary.

Place each poussin on a warm plate, pour a little gravy over it and put a spoonful of the herb bread sauce on one side. Serve with seasonal vegetables.

breasts of turkey with leeks, mushrooms and sliced potatoes

This dish is a far cry from those old turkey recipes that needed to be started off in the middle of the night in order to be ready for lunch. Young turkey breasts don't need a long cooking time – in fact, they can basically be treated like chicken.

Serves 4

2 turkey breasts, weighing about
500 g (1 lb 2 oz) each

Salt and freshly ground black pepper

6 tablespoons vegetable oil

140 g (5 oz) unsalted butter

200 g (8 oz) mushrooms, quartered

8–12 potatoes, peeled, parboiled
and sliced

200 g (8 oz) leeks, washed, trimmed and
cut into 1 cm (½ in) slices

FOR THE SAUCE

2 tablespoons finely chopped shallots

6 tablespoons dry white wine

½ teaspoon chopped fresh rosemary

140 g (5 oz) unsalted butter, chilled
and diced

Preheat-heat the oven to 200°C/400°F/Gas 6.

Trim the turkey breasts, removing any excess fat. Season generously with salt and pepper. Heat an ovenproof frying pan over a moderate heat. When hot, add 2 tablespoons of the oil and 25 g (1 oz) of the butter. Allow the butter to foam, then add the turkey breasts, skin-side down, and cook for 2–3 minutes or until the skin is nicely coloured. Turn over for 1 minute to seal the other side. Turn back onto the skin side and place in the oven for 20 minutes or until firm to the touch.

While the turkey is roasting, cook the vegetables. Pan-fry the mushrooms over a high heat in 50 g (2 oz) of the butter with a little salt and pepper. In another saucepan, fry the potatoes with 4 tablespoons of the oil and 25 g (2 oz) of the butter until golden brown. Cook the leeks in another saucepan, with the last 25 g (1 oz) butter, a good splash of water and a little salt and pepper, for about 3 minutes or until the water has evaporated and the leeks are tender. Keep all the vegetables warm.

Remove the turkey from the oven and allow to rest for 5 minutes in a warm place.

To make the sauce, tip any oil out of the turkey saucepan. Add the shallots to the saucepan and cook for 2 minutes over a gentle heat. Stir in the wine, scraping the bottom of the saucepan to loosen all the caramelized juices. Boil until almost all the wine has evaporated, then add 100 ml (3½ fl oz) of water and bring to the boil again. Add the rosemary and then gradually whisk in the diced butter.

To serve, spoon the vegetables attractively around the outside of four warm plates. Slice the turkey breasts and fan the slices in the centres of the plates. Top with a little sauce and serve.

roast spiced duck breasts with honey and cider vinegar

If you read between the lines in this recipe you'll realize that this is actually just a posh duck with sweet and sour sauce. No bad thing really, as most folks we know love a proper sweet 'n' sour. Get cooking!

Serves 4

2 large boneless Barbary duck breasts, weighing about 350 g (12 oz) each
Salt and freshly ground white pepper
Cayenne pepper

FOR THE SAUCE

4 tablespoons cider vinegar
½ apple, grated
2 teaspoons grated root ginger
100 ml (3½ fl oz) chicken stock
2 tablespoons honey
2 tablespoons soy sauce
A squeeze of lemon juice (optional)

Preheat the oven to 220°C/425°F/Gas 7.

To prepare and cook the duck, trim the duck breasts and lightly score the skin side with a sharp knife. Season the skin side with salt, turn the breasts over and season with salt, pepper and a little cayenne pepper.

Place the duck breasts, skin-side down, in a hot, dry, ovenproof frying pan. Let them cook over moderate heat for about 5 minutes or until the skin is nicely golden and crisp. Pour off any excess fat, turn the breasts over and cook for another minute, just to seal the other side. Turn them back onto their skin sides and place the saucepan in the preheated oven for about 4 minutes for medium rare, 6 minutes for medium or 10 minutes for well done. Remove the duck breasts from the saucepan, and let them rest while you make the sauce.

To make the sauce, pour off any fat left in the saucepan. Add the vinegar, apple and ginger, and boil until the liquid has almost evaporated. Add the chicken stock, honey and soy sauce and bring back to the boil. Boil for about 2 minutes to thicken to a nice sauce consistency that will coat the back of a spoon. Taste the sauce and add a squeeze of lemon juice if necessary.

To serve, slice the duck breasts thinly and arrange on warm plates. Pour over a little sauce and serve at once.

peppered duck breasts with wild mushrooms and cream

This is basically just a pepper steak dish except that it uses duck breasts. If you don't enjoy duck skin, you can remove it by simply pulling it away from the breast. Release any stuck bits by nicking them with a sharp knife.

Serves 4

4 female boneless Barbary duck breasts

2–3 tablespoons cracked black peppercorns

Salt

50 ml (2 fl oz) cognac

100 ml (3½ fl oz) light gravy or stock

100 ml (3½ fl oz) double cream

8 flatleaf parsley sprigs, to garnish

FOR THE MUSHROOM MIXTURE

100 g (4 oz) shiitake mushrooms

100 g (4 oz) oyster mushrooms

30 g (generous 1 oz) dried black trumpet mushrooms, soaked and drained

30 ml (1 fl oz) light olive oil

2 tablespoons butter

100 g (4 oz) fresh spinach

Trim the duck breasts and lightly score the skin sides with a sharp knife. Spread the cracked peppercorns on the duck breasts, pressing them into the breasts. Season with salt.

Heat a large frying pan over a moderate heat and place the duck breasts in it, skin-side down. Let them cook for 5 minutes or until the skin is nicely golden and crisp. Turn the breasts over, and cook for another 4 minutes. Remove the duck breasts from the pan and keep warm.

Pour off the fat, and deglaze the saucepan with the cognac. Add the gravy or stock, stirring well to scrape up the caramelized juices. Add the cream and simmer to reduce to a sauce consistency that will coat the back of a spoon.

To make the mushroom mixture, fry the mushrooms in the oil and 1 tablespoon of the butter. Fry the spinach in the remaining butter. Mix the two together.

To serve, spoon the mushroom mixture onto four warm plates. Slice the duck breasts and arrange them on top. Surround with the sauce and garnish with sprigs of parsley.

roast goose with traditional sage and onion stuffing

There is no doubt that goose is delicious, but it can be disappointing because of its low yield of meat – so do allow 750 g (1 lb 10 oz) per person. This recipe will give you delicious, light gravy that really suits the richness of the goose meat.

Serves 6

Salt and freshly ground black pepper

1 oven-ready goose, weighing about 4 kg (9 lb)

500 ml (18 fl oz) Brown Chicken Stock (see page 232) or water

Unsalted butter, chilled and diced

Tangy Beetroot Purée (see page 166), to serve (optional)

FOR THE SAGE AND ONION STUFFING

3 tablespoons butter

750 g (1 lb 10 oz) onions, minced or finely chopped

Salt and freshly ground black pepper

30 fresh sage leaves, chopped

1 goose liver

175 g (6 oz) sausage meat

2 egg yolks

175 g (6 oz) fresh breadcrumbs

A small handful of chopped fresh parsley

Preheat the oven to 220°C/425°F/Gas 7.

First prepare the sage and onion stuffing. Melt the butter in a large saucepan and sweat the onions over a low heat with a pinch of salt for about 10 minutes. Add the sage and liver and cook for a further 2 minutes. Tip the onion mixture into a large bowl and allow to cool slightly. Mix in the sausagemeat, egg yolks, breadcrumbs and parsley, and season generously with salt and pepper.

Season the goose lightly inside and out and insert the stuffing into the body cavity. Tie the legs together tightly and prick the skin with a toothpick or trussing needle to allow the fat to escape during cooking. Lay the goose in a deep roasting tin and cook in the oven for 30 minutes.

Reduce the temperature to 150°C/300°F/Gas 2 and cook for a further 2½ hours, basting the goose with its own fat about every 20 minutes.

Remove the goose from the oven, place on a warm serving plate and cover with foil to rest for about 15 minutes. Pour off the fat from the roasting tin, saving all the dark roasting juices. Deglaze the tin with the stock or water, scraping all the caramelized juices off the bottom of the tin. Strain the juices into a clean saucepan and boil until reduced to about 300 ml (½ pint). Finally, whisk in 1–2 tablespoons of butter and check and adjust the seasoning to taste.

To carve the goose, remove the legs and breasts first. To do this, cut the skin where the legs meet the breasts. Turn the goose on its side. Hold the drumstick with a clean cloth and pull the entire leg down towards the back. The thigh bone should pop out of its socket so that you only have to cut any awkward tendons to release the leg. Repeat with the other side.

Cut through the legs to release the drumsticks, and cut each of the thighs in half, parallel to the thigh bone. This will give you six leg portions.

To release the breasts, cut along each side of the breast bone. You can then easily push the breasts away from the bone with your knife or fingers. Set the breasts on a cutting board and cut each one into 6 pieces, as required. Allow two slices of breast meat and one leg portion per person.

Serve with a generous scoop of the stuffing and a drizzle of the gravy, and some beetroot purée, if liked. Serve the remaining gravy on the side.

breasts of pigeon with sage and black pepper

This is really a recipe for wild pigeon, which are widely available in Ireland. The meat from the wild birds is absolutely stunning, but you must be sure to cook them quite slowly and to keep the meat fairly rare.

Serves 4

4 pigeons, skin on
2 tablespoons light olive oil
2 tablespoons finely chopped onion
2 tablespoons finely chopped carrot
2 tablespoons finely chopped celery
1 garlic clove, crushed
1 bay leaf
4 juniper berries
8 peppercorns
125 ml (4 fl oz) red wine
250 ml (9 fl oz) Brown Chicken Stock (see page 232)
1/2 teaspoon cracked black peppercorns
1 teaspoon chopped fresh sage
2 tablespoons butter
Salt and freshly ground black pepper
Carrot and Parsnip Mash (see page 167), to serve
Buttered spinach or cabbage, to serve
4 fresh sage sprigs, to garnish

With a sharp-pointed knife cut the breasts away from the pigeon carcasses, keeping your knife towards the bones all the time. Trim the breast fillets into a nice shape and set to one side.

Chop the carcasses and legs with a heavy knife and sauté in 1 tablespoon of the oil in a large frying pan, until well browned. Now add the vegetables, garlic, bay leaf, juniper berries and the eight peppercorns, and cook for another 5 minutes. Deglaze the saucepan with the wine, scraping the bottom of the saucepan to release all the tasty bits. Reduce the wine until it has almost disappeared, then add the chicken stock. Bring to the boil and simmer for 15 minutes.

Strain through a fine sieve into a clean bowl and stir in the cracked peppercorns, sage and 1 tablespoon of butter. Taste for seasoning, adding more salt if necessary. Keep the sauce in a warm place.

To cook the pigeon breasts, melt the remaining butter with the remaining oil in a large sauté saucepan. Season the breasts with salt and pepper. When the butter is foaming add the pigeon breasts, skin-side down. Adjust the heat so that the delicate breasts don't cook too fast. They should brown slowly, without becoming crispy. Cook for about 4 minutes, then turn over for another 2 minutes for medium rare. When cooked, remove to a warm plate to rest for 2 minutes.

To serve, remove the skin from the breasts with a sharp knife and slice each one in two. Place a serving of the mash in the centre of four plates. Divide the buttered spinach or cabbage into four portions and place on top of the mash, then place two slices of breast on top of the vegetables. Spoon a little of the sauce over and around and garnish with a sprig of sage.

roast partridges with bacon, garlic and thyme

This is a great recipe for most game birds. Try it with pigeon, pheasant or grouse.
Just be aware that the cooking times will vary depending on the size of the bird.

Serves 4

4 young oven-ready partridges, livers
reserved if available

Salt and freshly ground black pepper

20 garlic cloves, blanched for 10 minutes

8 fresh thyme sprigs

12 rashers of smoked bacon

4 tablespoons light olive oil

6 tablespoons butter

4 shallots, sliced

500 ml (18 fl oz) Brown Chicken Stock
(see page 232)

Preheat the oven to 220°C/425°F/Gas 7.

Season the partridges inside and out with salt and pepper and stuff 5 garlic cloves and a sprig of thyme inside each bird. Drape 3 rashers of bacon over each bird and secure in place with string or toothpicks.

Place a large ovenproof frying pan in the oven and heat the oil and 2 tablespoons of the butter until the butter is foaming and very hot. Remove the pan from the oven, add the partridges and fry them briefly on all sides. Place the birds on their sides, return the pan to the oven, and roast the partridges for 8–10 minutes on each side. Remove from the oven, take the birds out of the pan and allow them to rest for 5 minutes.

Meanwhile pour off excess fat from the saucepan, then sweat the shallots in the pan with a little of the butter. Untie the birds and place on a cutting board. Remove the garlic cloves and bacon and set aside on a baking sheet. Remove the legs and breasts from the partridges and place them on the baking sheet with the garlic and bacon. Keep in a warm place. Chop the carcasses and the livers, if available, and add to the shallots. Cook gently for a few minutes. Add the stock, 4 sprigs of thyme (reserving a few leaves) and 2 of the garlic cloves. Simmer for 5 minutes, then strain through a fine sieve into a clean saucepan. Boil until the liquid reduces to a nice sauce consistency (it should coat the back of a spoon). Whisk in the remaining butter and a few of the reserved leaves of thyme, and season with salt and pepper.

Pop the birds back in the oven for 2 minutes to allow the legs and breasts and garlic cloves to heat through.

To serve, arrange two legs and two pieces of breast on each warm plate. Pour over a little sauce and garnish with the roasted bacon, garlic and the remaining thyme leaves. Serve at once.

beef chop with red wine

A beef chop is, of course, just a small rib roast on the bone. The French call it *côte du boeuf*. In Ireland we like to call a spade a spade, so it is a beef chop. You can think of it as a steak cut four times thicker than normal. It develops a beautiful caramelized crust and yet stays beautifully rare in the middle.

Serves 4

1 fore-rib of beef on the bone, weighing about 1.25 kg (2 lb 12 oz), with chine bone removed

½ tablespoon salt

1 tablespoon cracked black peppercorns

2 tablespoons light olive oil

2 tablespoons butter

6 shallots, finely sliced into rounds and soaked in 250 ml (9 fl oz) good-quality red wine for 1 hour

4–6 tablespoons meat gravy or stock

2 tablespoons unsalted butter, chilled and diced

Salt and freshly ground black pepper

A pinch of sugar

Cheesy Yorkshire Puddings (see page 166), to serve

Sprigs of watercress, to garnish (optional)

Preheat the oven to 240°C/475°F/Gas 9.

Ask your butcher for the third-rib roast, situated where the sirloin meets the rib eye. Trim off any bones except the actual rib bone itself. Trim meat and sinew from the top of the rib to give an attractive chop presentation. Before cooking, take the meat out of the fridge and allow it to come to room temperature.

Season the beef with the ½ teaspoon salt and the peppercorns. Heat a large, heavy, ovenproof frying pan over a high heat, add the olive oil and butter and allow to brown lightly. Now add the beef and brown it carefully all over. Place in the oven and cook for 15 minutes for rare, or approximately 25 minutes for medium to well done, turning occasionally.

Remove the beef to a plate, and cover with foil to rest for 5–10 minutes while you make the sauce.

Pour the excess fat from the saucepan, then add the shallots and wine to the pan. Allow the wine to boil vigorously until it has reduced by two-thirds. Now add the meat gravy or stock and any juices from the beef chop. Bring to a simmer, then gradually whisk in the butter. Taste for seasoning, adding salt, pepper and a pinch of sugar if necessary.

To serve, place the chop on a carving board, and carve it downwards into eight slices. Season lightly with salt. Reassemble the chop on a warm serving dish, top with a little of the sauce and garnish with sprigs of watercress, if you wish. Serve with cheesy yorkshire puddings.

warm steak salad with anchovy and caper vinaigrette

A wonderful, light main-course dish, perfect for the barbecue season, this is Paul's favourite way to eat steak. Cut it extra thick, char it well, then slice it. If you don't fancy the anchovies, substitute olives. Serve with home-made chips.

Serves 6

12 small or 6 medium leeks

6 small red onions, cut into quarters

Light olive oil, for brushing

Salt and freshly ground black pepper

6 fresh free-range organic eggs

1.5 kg (3 lb 5 oz) piece of well-hung sirloin steak

Mixed salad leaves, to serve

1 tablespoon chopped fresh flatleaf parsley, to garnish

FOR THE ANCHOVY AND CAPER VINAIGRETTE

3 tablespoons white wine vinegar

1 tablespoon Dijon mustard

200 ml (7 fl oz) olive oil

2 tablespoons finely chopped shallots

2 tablespoons capers, rinsed and finely chopped

2 tablespoons roughly chopped anchovies

1/2 tablespoon cracked black peppercorns

Salt and freshly ground black pepper (optional)

First make the anchovy and caper vinaigrette, whisk together the vinegar, mustard and oil in a small bowl. Add the shallots, capers, anchovies and peppercorns. Taste for seasoning and add salt and pepper if necessary.

Preheat the barbecue or grill to high.

Blanch the leeks in boiling, salted water for about 7 minutes, or until tender. Refresh in plenty of cold water and squeeze out as much of the water as possible. Brush the leeks and onions with a little oil and season with salt and pepper. Set aside.

Bring a medium-sized saucepan of salted water to the boil, gently add the eggs and hard-boil for 8 minutes. Plunge the eggs into cold water and, when cool enough to handle, peel carefully. Set aside.

Trim off any excess fat from the steak and cut into 3 cm (1¼ in) slices. Season well, then brush with oil. Cook the steaks on the barbecue, a griddle pan or under the grill until well charred on both sides. When quite blackened the steaks should still be rare inside. Cook for another 5 minutes for medium, or another 10 minutes for well done. Leave the steaks to rest on a warm plate, covered lightly with foil.

Meanwhile, cook the leeks and onions on the barbecue or under the grill for about 5 minutes, or until charred and tender.

To serve, cut the hard-boiled eggs into quarters, lengthways. Place some of the salad leaves in the middle of each plate and add the egg quarters, leeks and onions. Slice the steaks into thick pieces and arrange the pieces on top of the salad, then spoon over some of the vinaigrette. Garnish with the parsley and serve at once.

barbecued rack of pork with grilled vegetables and herbes de provence

This is a very tasty recipe for pork. The trick is the salt marinade which cures the meat ever so slightly. Cooking the pork on the barbecue with lovely fresh herbs makes it even better of course. If you find that the bones on the rack start to burn, cover them with foil.

Serves 4

1 rack of pork, weighing about 900 g (2 lb), with 4–5 rib bones
Sea salt and freshly ground black pepper
125 ml (4 fl oz) light olive oil

FOR THE *HERBES DE PROVENCE*
2 tablespoons chopped fresh parsley
1 tablespoon chopped fresh thyme
1 tablespoon chopped fresh rosemary
1 teaspoon chopped fresh sage
1 teaspoon dried oregano
2 bay leaves, crushed

FOR THE DRESSING
250 ml (9 fl oz) virgin olive oil
Juice of 1 lemon
1 teaspoon salt
1 teaspoon cracked black peppercorns

FOR THE VEGETABLES
About 900 g (2 lb) mixed vegetables, such as aubergines, courgettes, red onions, mushrooms, leeks, carrots and potatoes
125 ml (4 fl oz) olive oil
Salt and freshly ground black pepper

Trim the rack of pork of skin and clean the meat from between the bones to expose the bones, nice and cleanly. Mix together all the *herbes de provence* ingredients. Rub the salt, pepper and 2 tablespoons of the herbs into the pork rack and then put into the fridge, covered, for at least 4–8 hours or preferably overnight.

About 50 minutes before eating, light the barbecue or preheat the grill to medium-high. Take the pork out of the fridge, drain off any juices and lightly pat it dry. When the barbecue is hot, drizzle a little oil over the pork and put it on a part that is moderately hot. Alternatively, place under the grill. Cook for about 30 minutes, turning it and basting it with a little oil from time to time. Leave to rest for about 5–10 minutes to allow the juices to settle.

Place all the ingredients for the dressing in a small bowl. Add 2 tablespoons of the herb mixture and allow to stand while you prepare the vegetables. Turn the grill to high, if using.

Cut the vegetables into attractive shapes and sizes, but make sure that they are not so small that they will fall through the barbecue racks. Toss the vegetables in the oil and sprinkle them with the remaining herbs and a little salt and pepper.

About 10 minutes before eating, start to cook the vegetables on the hottest part of the barbecue or under the grill. Watch them very carefully, turning them once or twice before removing them to a warm plate.

To serve, carve the rack of pork into four large cutlets. Arrange the vegetables on four plates and put a cutlet in the centre of each. Drizzle the dressing over the entire plates and serve.

marinated loin of pork with thyme

In this dish we give the pork roast a long marinade so that it takes on a taste similar to wild boar. This is one of the first recipes Paul ever cooked (even before he turned professional) and one that we still come back to.

Serves 4

1.25 kg (2 lb 12 oz) rack of pork

2 tablespoons vegetable oil

2 tablespoons unsalted butter, chilled and diced

Salt and freshly ground black pepper

FOR THE MARINADE

2 garlic cloves, crushed

1 carrot, diced

1 onion, diced

100 ml (3½ fl oz) red wine vinegar

300 ml (½ pint) red wine

4 tablespoons olive oil

1 teaspoon black peppercorns

1 tablespoon salt

1 teaspoon sugar

2 bay leaves

4 fresh thyme sprigs

12 juniper berries

Remove the skin of the pork if your butcher has not done so.

Place all the marinade ingredients in a large saucepan and bring to the boil. Simmer for 2 minutes and then allow to cool. Place the pork in a deep, non-reactive (ceramic or stainless-steel) container and pour the marinade over the pork. Cover with clingfilm and chill for 48 hours, turning every 6 hours.

After 48 hours, preheat the oven to 200°C/400°F/Gas 6. Remove the pork from the marinade and dry with a clean cloth. Reserve the marinade. Heat a large frying pan over a high heat, add the oil and brown the pork well on all sides. Transfer it to a roasting tin and roast in the preheated oven for 40 minutes.

Remove the pork from the oven and place the pork to rest on a large plate, lightly covered with foil.

Drain excess fat from the tin and deglaze it using 200 ml (7 fl oz) of the marinade. Scrape the bottom of the tin with a wooden spoon to loosen all the delicious caramelized juices. Strain into a clean saucepan and boil until you have reduced the liquid by about half. Now whisk in the butter and adjust the seasoning to taste.

Carve the pork into equal portions and serve with a little sauce.

ulster fry with steam-fried eggs

'What on earth is a steam-fried egg?' we hear you say. Paul developed this technique when he was a health-conscious student and had never yet been near a professional kitchen. Amazingly enough, of all the recipes we have cooked on telly over the years this one still draws the most comments. 'Love the way you fried those eggs!', 'The only way I ever cook an egg now!' We are delighted you love our eggs, but have to confess the reason we chose this recipe was to highlight the way we incorporate the potato breads and soda farls into our Ulster breakfasts. You must try the breads, they are even better than the eggs.

Serves 4

2 rashers of streaky bacon
2 tablespoons vegetable oil
4 rashers of back bacon
1 ripe tomato, halved
Salt and freshly ground black pepper
1 Irish Soda Farl (see page 228)
2 quarters of Potato Bread (see page 228)
1 teaspoon unsalted butter
4 fresh free-range organic eggs

Fry the streaky bacon in a large frying pan with the oil. When almost cooked, add the back bacon and the tomato halves, seasoned with salt and pepper. Cook until the streaky rashers are crisp, the back bacon cooked but not dried out and the tomatoes are just beginning to soften. Transfer them all to a warm oven, reserving the fat in the saucepan.

Cut the soda farl in half lengthways and then cut each side in half again, ending up with four pieces. Cut the potato breads into two pieces. Dip the pieces in the fat left in the pan, let them soak it up a little and then drain away any excess. Dry-fry the pieces of bread gently until they are starting to crisp up. Remove them from the saucepan and reserve in the oven.

To fry the eggs, allow the teaspoon of butter to melt in a non-stick frying pan until it is sizzling. Crack the eggs carefully into the saucepan, add 2 tablespoons of water and a little salt and cover the saucepan. Allow the eggs to cook slowly for about 2 minutes or until they are done to your taste.

Serve at once on warm plates, dividing the bacon, breads, tomatoes and eggs between them.

roast kassler with cabbage and potatoes

This is a simple one-pan dish of humble origins, taking inspiration from age-old cabbage and bacon recipes. The smoked, German-style ham, kassler, perfumes the cabbage and potatoes with rich smoky aromas. If you can't find kassler a smoked bacon loin will do.

Serves 6–8

1 kg (2 lb 4 oz) potatoes, peeled and quartered

450 g (1 lb) Savoy cabbage, outer leaves removed, cored and roughly chopped

1 kg (2 lb 4 oz) boned kassler or smoked bacon loin

2 tablespoons unsalted butter

Salt

FOR THE SAUCE

25 g (1 oz) unsalted butter

1 tablespoon plain white flour

600 ml (1 pint) cold chicken stock

50 ml (2 fl oz) port or Madeira

1–3 tablespoons Dijon mustard

Salt and freshly ground black pepper

Preheat the oven to 200°C/400°F/Gas 6.

To parboil the potatoes, place them in a large saucepan, cover with cold, salted water and bring to the boil. Simmer for 5 minutes and then drain the potatoes in a colander. This parboiling helps to remove moisture and surface starch that would make the potatoes stick to the roasting tin.

Parboil the cabbage in a large saucepan of lightly salted water for 2 minutes. Drain in a colander, refresh in cold water and then squeeze dry with your hands.

Place the kassler in a large roasting tin and put in the oven. Roast for about 10 minutes and then add the butter. When the butter has melted, add the potatoes. Roast for 20 minutes, turning the kassler and potatoes occasionally. Push the potatoes and kassler to one side and add the cabbage. Season the potatoes and cabbage with salt. Roast for another 10 minutes, turning all the ingredients in the smoky butter.

While the kassler is roasting, make the sauce. Melt the butter in a small saucepan and add the flour. Cook for 2 minutes, stirring occasionally. Take off the heat, and whisk in the chicken stock. Whisk until smooth, then return to the heat and simmer for 20 minutes, stirring occasionally.

Remove the kassler from the oven. Check that the potatoes and cabbage are properly cooked and transfer them to a warm serving plate. Slice the kassler, arrange on the cabbage, and keep warm while you finish the sauce.

Deglaze the juices in the roasting tin with the port or Madeira and add to the sauce. Whisk in the mustard and season carefully with salt and pepper. Serve the sauce separately.

peppered leg of venison with hot and sour cabbage

A well-hung haunch of venison is just as nice to eat as the loin or fillet. The technique used here for separating the leg muscles means you are left with sinew-free 'loin' from the leg.

Serves 6

1 haunch of venison, weighing about 2.5 kg (5 lb 8 oz)

Cracked black peppercorns

2 tablespoons butter

1 tablespoon vegetable oil

Salt and freshly ground black pepper

FOR THE HOT AND SOUR CABBAGE

2 tablespoons butter

1 red cabbage, finely sliced

50 ml (2 fl oz) sherry wine vinegar

Salt, sugar and freshly ground white pepper to taste

2 apples, peeled, cored and chopped

2 tablespoons raisins

1 tablespoon chopped fresh root ginger

FOR THE SAUCE

50 ml (2 fl oz) sherry wine vinegar

50 ml (2 fl oz) meat stock or gravy (optional)

300 ml (½ pint) double cream

Preheat the oven to 190°C/375°F/Gas 5.

First cook the hot and sour cabbage. Melt the butter in a large, heavy-based flameproof casserole. Add the cabbage, vinegar and salt to taste. Cover and cook over a low heat for about 1 hour.

Stir in the apples, raisins, ginger and sugar to taste, and cook slowly for another 30 minutes. Finally, add some pepper and check the seasoning to see if it needs more sugar or salt.

Meanwhile, cook the venison. Trim the outside of the haunch to remove any sinew and fat. Work carefully to see that you don't remove too much. Separate the large muscles, one at a time, and place them to one side. Reserve the trimmings, shin and very small muscles for another use. Roll the large muscles in the peppercorns and season with salt.

Heat a large frying pan and fry the pieces of venison in the butter and oil until they have a nice colour on all sides. Then place them in the oven for 5 minutes for medium rare or 8 minutes for medium to well done.

Remove the venison pieces from the saucepan and allow them to rest in a warm place while you make the sauce.

To make the sauce, pour off any fat from the saucepan and deglaze the pan with the sherry vinegar. Scrape the bottom of the saucepan with a wooden spoon to loosen all the delicious, caramelized juices. Reduce the vinegar to 1 tablespoon, then add the meat stock or gravy, if using, and the cream. Reduce the liquid by boiling quickly until it has reached a sauce consistency that coats the back of a spoon. Season with salt and pepper.

To serve, divide the piping hot cabbage between six warm plates, slice the venison pieces and arrange the slices neatly on top of the cabbage. Pour over a little of the sauce and serve.

loin of venison with bacon and irish whiskey cream

This is quite a simple dish but it has an intriguing, deep flavour from the spice mixture and the bacon. At work we often omit the cream in the sauce and instead just serve it with a creamy accompaniment such as Creamy Potato Gratin (see page 162) or Champ (see page 160).

Serves 6

500 g (1 lb 2 oz) boneless venison loin, well trimmed

12 rashers of streaky bacon

3 tablespoons Irish whiskey

1 tablespoon vegetable oil

1 tablespoon butter

Roast vegetables or Creamy Potato Gratin (see page 162) or Champ (see page 160), to serve

FOR THE SPICE MIXTURE

6 juniper berries

2 cloves

$1/4$ teaspoon dried thyme

2 teaspoons black peppercorns

$1/2$ teaspoon salt

FOR THE IRISH WHISKEY CREAM

250 ml (9 fl oz) Brown Chicken Stock (see page 232)

125 ml (4 fl oz) double cream

Grind the ingredients for the spices together using a pestle and mortar or in a small coffee grinder.

Slice the venison loin into 12 even-sized medallions and sprinkle the meat evenly with the spice mixture. Drizzle 2 tablespoons of the whiskey over them. Wrap a slice of streaky bacon around the circumference of each medallion and fix it in place with a cocktail stick.

Fry the medallions over a high heat in a heavy-based frying pan with the oil and butter. Fry for about 2 minutes on each side, then turn each medallion onto its circumference to crisp up the bacon a little. When all the bacon is lightly crisped all round, pour off any excess fat and add the remaining 1 tablespoon of whiskey to the saucepan. Carefully ignite it to flambé the venison. Remove the meat, and allow it to rest in a warm place while finishing the sauce.

To make the Irish whiskey cream, add the stock to the saucepan and boil over a high heat until the sauce consistency preferred is reached. Add the cream and return to the boil.

Place two of the medallions in the centre of each warm plate, and pour the sauce around them. Serve with roast vegetables, potato gratin or champ.

warm game tart with roast winter vegetables and green peppercorns

For us this dish conjures up thoughts of grand country houses, large fires and winter evenings. Paul reckons it would be a great alternative to turkey on Christmas day.

Serves 6

200 g (8 oz) Puff Pastry (see pages 233–4)
Plain white flour, for dusting
1 egg yolk, mixed with 1 teaspoon water

FOR THE FILLING

300 g (10 oz) game meat, such as pheasant legs, venison shoulder, hare, pigeon, well trimmed
140 g (5 oz) good-quality pork sausage meat, from a butcher
75 g (2½ oz) streaky bacon
75 g (2½ oz) pork-back fat
1 tablespoon brandy
1 shallot, chopped
1 garlic clove, chopped
1 tablespoon chopped fresh parsley
1 tablespoon chopped fresh thyme or ½ teaspoon dried thyme
1 teaspoon freshly ground black pepper
½ teaspoon salt

FOR THE SAUCE

150 ml (¼ pint) meat gravy or good brown stock, e.g. Brown Chicken Stock (see page 232)
150 ml (¼ pint) double cream
2 tablespoons Irish whiskey or cognac
1 tablespoon green peppercorns, lightly crushed
Salt

First make the filling. Check that all the game meat is well trimmed, and ensure that it has no discoloured bits or tough sinews. Slice the meat and fat into manageable pieces (about 7.5 x 2.5 x 1 cm/3 x 1 x ½ in). Combine the filling ingredients in a bowl and mix them roughly. Put this mixture through the coarse blade of your mincer attachment (if you don't have one you could ask your butcher to do this, or chop the meat by hand very finely). Beat the meat well with a wooden spoon, or mix it by hand, to ensure that it is blended thoroughly. Form into a ball and place in the fridge.

On a floured surface, roll out the pastry into two large rectangles; each sheet should be about 30 x 30 cm (12 x 12 in) and no thicker than 3 mm (⅛ in). Chill these for at least 20 minutes.

When they are nice and cold, take one sheet from the fridge and cut out a large (about 24 cm/9½ in) circle. The easiest way to accomplish this is to use an overturned bowl or plate as a guide. Brush this base completely with the egg wash, taking care not to let any wash drip over the sides.

Place the filling in the centre of the base and, with your hands, pat it into an even dome shape. There should be a perimeter of at least 4–6 cm (1½–2½ in) of pastry around the filling. Take the other sheet of pastry from the fridge and quickly reapply egg wash to the perimeter of the base before carefully laying the second sheet on top. Using your hands, gently pat this sheet into place. You need to shape the pastry over the filling and seal the two edges together. Try not to leave any big air pockets inside, and try to not stretch the top sheet or it will lose shape during cooking.

Brush the whole top of the tart with the egg wash, making sure none of the wash drips over the edges, and then cut the edges so that they are even with each other. Pierce a small hole in the centre of the top of the tart to release steam during cooking, and decorate however you like, using the back of a knife, the tines of a fork or even a toothpick. Chill in the fridge for 20 minutes.

Preheat the oven to 190°C/375°F/Gas 5.

Bake the tart for about 30 minutes, until golden brown.

FOR THE VEGETABLES

900 g (2 lb) assortment of carrots, potatoes, Brussels sprouts, mushrooms, baby onions, etc. (use what you like or have available)

125 g (4½ oz) butter

Salt and freshly ground black pepper

To make the sauce, simply boil the gravy or stock with the cream until it has thickened to a sauce consistency that coats the back of a spoon. Add the whiskey or cognac and the green peppercorns. Simmer over a low heat for 1–2 minutes, then check the seasoning and add salt as needed. Keep warm.

To prepare the vegetables, boil or steam them until they are just cooked. Allow them to cool slightly.

Heat the butter in a large casserole until it foams and is just turning brown. Throw all the vegetables in at once and allow them to cook gently in the butter for about 5 minutes. Turn them carefully from time to time to ensure that they are coated with the butter, then season with salt and pepper.

To serve, bring the tart to the table with the vegetables either surrounding it on the plate, or in their own serving bowl, and pass the sauce separately.

Stews were originally developed as one-pot dishes to save fuel. (Interestingly enough, the Chinese went the other way and developed super-quick stir-fried dishes to save energy!) Also, long, slow cooking with liquid was the only way to make cheaper leftover cuts of meat edible. Paul reckons there is a certain amount of romance to a stew. Imagine a big, black pot sitting at the edge of the fire, just barely ticking over, being policed lovingly by a hard-working mother, daughter or granny. Stews conjure up just such wonderful images, not to mention hungry kids with rosy cheeks, men coming in from the fields frozen and wet through, happy gatherings by the hearth or fire, lots of 'craic', wonderful aromas, warmth and friendship. That sits well in any culture, doesn't it?

The secret of a good stew or braise is to understand the meat you're cooking as well as the technique. Each cut will take a different amount of time to cook, so, if you add vegetables near the end of the cooking, your timing needs to be good or they can simmer away to mush. It is better to rely on tasting, poking and prodding to know when your meat is cooked, the clock will only ever be a rough guide. Try to develop this skill by carefully removing a piece of meat and either tasting it or pushing it gently to see whether it's tender or starting to come away from the bone. All the best cooks do this.

The last 30 minutes of cooking are the most important. This is when the meat will either be cooked or not, but be careful not to overcook it as it could become stringy and dry, and can even get to the stage of literally falling to bits. Be careful not to cook it too fast either, especially in the later stages, when it is most fragile. Paul sometimes takes a stew off a little early so that it can finish cooking through its own heat.

Remember to taste carefully. If your braising liquid is bland towards the end of the cooking period, then your stew or braise will be bland. With this technique all the flavours blend together via the liquid. The liquid will absorb the flavours of the meat and also transfer the tastes of the aromatics and seasonings to the meat. One word of caution – don't over-season the liquid as it will reduce through cooking and become quite intensified.

Once you are confident with stews and braises you will be free to make up your own recipes from whatever is at hand, or in season. This is when it becomes very satisfying. You will churn out success after success, and your family or guests will just keep coming back for more.

stews and braised dishes

irish stew

Is there a more famous dish in the world than Irish stew? We guess it is so renowned because of its simplicity and because it is so satisfying. Every country has in its culinary history a basic one-pot dish – maybe it is an idea that is just too tasty and wholesome to pass up. At any rate, this is Paul's current favourite. Of course, you need to be in the right mood to enjoy a good stew – but on a wet day (or night) in winter in Ireland there really is nothing more warming, delicious and filling.

Serves 4

900 g (2 lb) boneless shoulder (or neck) of lamb, trimmed and cubed

Salt

225 g (8 oz) potatoes, peeled and cut into chunks

225 g (8 oz) carrots, washed, trimmed and coarsely sliced

225 g (8 oz) leeks, cut in coarse slices

225 g (8 oz) baby onions

2 fresh thyme sprigs

250 ml (9 fl oz) double cream

1 tablespoon unsalted butter

A handful of fresh parsley leaves, blanched and refreshed

Place the lamb in a heavy flameproof casserole with 1.2 litres (2 pints) of water and a little salt. Bring to the boil – just – and skim off any scum and fat, then simmer for 30 minutes.

Add half the potatoes and simmer for another 30 minutes. Stir quite vigorously to break up the potatoes. Add the rest of the potatoes and the remaining vegetables and the thyme. Simmer for another 30 minutes, or until the meat and vegetables are tender.

Add the cream, butter and parsley, then reheat quickly and serve.

braised lamb shanks with pearl barley and root vegetables

This dish could almost be called Irish stew. Indeed, it is a wonderful alternative. Notice that there is actually very little barley in the recipe – it is simply another ingredient in the rich vegetable broth.

Serves 4

4 lamb shanks

1 tablespoon vegetable oil

2 tablespoons pearl barley

300 ml (½ pint) lamb stock or water

1 fresh thyme sprig or ½ teaspoon dried thyme

1 fresh parsley sprig

Salt and freshly ground black pepper

140 g (5 oz) carrots, roughly chopped

1 large leek, washed, trimmed and cut into 8 pieces

4 small potatoes, peeled and quartered

2 small onions, quartered

A handful of fresh parsley leaves, blanched and refreshed

Preheat the oven to 160°C/325°F/Gas 3.

Ask your butcher to trim off any excess fat from the shanks and to remove the knuckles from the shanks. Heat the oil in a large frying pan over a high heat. Fry the lamb shanks until nicely coloured on all sides. Transfer them to a large braising dish and add the barley, stock or water, herbs and 1 teaspoon salt. Cover tightly with foil and a lid and cook in the oven for 1½ hours.

Remove the braising dish from the oven and add the vegetables and a little more water if needed. Season the vegetables lightly with salt and pepper, then cover the braising dish and return it to the oven for another hour.

Remove the dish from the oven and check that the lamb is moist and almost falling off the bone. If you think that it's not quite ready, return it to the oven for another 15 minutes. Transfer the lamb to a warm serving plate and cover while you finish the braised vegetables.

To finish the vegetables place the braising dish on the hob and bring back to a simmer, adding more water if needed to give a nice consistency. Add the parsley, and check and adjust the seasoning to taste.

To serve, ladle the braised vegetables onto four warm plates and place a lamb shank on top of each serving.

braised lamb shanks with thyme and roast carrots

How did the lowly lamb shank become such a worldwide culinary star? Because it is gorgeous, that's how! All those sinews and ligaments in those strong muscles literally melt in the braising process to give that magnificent rich texture and deep flavours.

Serves 4

4 lamb shanks

2 tablespoons light olive oil

4 carrots, cut into 2.5 cm (1 in) chunks

12 baby onions, peeled

3 fresh thyme sprigs

Salt and freshly ground pepper

2 tablespoons butter

1 tablespoon chopped fresh parsley

1 teaspoon fresh thyme leaves

Champ (see page 160), to serve (optional)

Preheat the oven to 150°C/300°F/Gas 2.

Trim the shanks of excess fat and saw off the knuckles (or ask your butcher to do this). In a heavy-based flameproof casserole, brown the shanks on all sides in the oil. Remove the shanks and brown the carrots and onions. When the vegetables are golden brown, remove them and reserve. Return the shanks to the casserole, with the thyme sprigs and 2 tablespoons of water, and season with a little salt. Cover and place in the oven. Cook the shanks for 1½ hours, turning occasionally.

Now return the carrots and onions to the casserole and cook for another hour. Remove the shanks and vegetables and keep warm.

Strain the cooking juices into a small saucepan. Using a ladle, or spoon, remove any visible fat from the top of the juices. Now boil the liquid until it has a light sauce consistency. Remove it from the heat and stir in the butter, parsley and thyme leaves. Taste for seasoning and add salt and pepper as necessary.

To serve, season the shanks lightly with salt and arrange on warm plates. Surround with the carrots and onions and pour over the sauce. Serve with mashed potatoes or champ.

slow-roast shoulder of lamb with rosemary and garlic

When this dish is cooked carefully it is just stunning. The trick is to caramelize the cooking juices onto the meat to give a tasty glaze. If the casserole dish gets too dry, moisten it with a little red wine.

Serves 6–8

1.25 kg (2 lb 12 oz) boneless shoulder of lamb, shank removed

Salt and freshly ground black pepper

2 tablespoons light olive oil

2 tablespoons chopped onion

2 tablespoons chopped carrot

2 tablespoons chopped celery

125 ml (4 fl oz) red wine

1 tablespoon chopped fresh rosemary

1 tablespoon butter

New potatoes, to serve (optional)

FOR THE MARINADE

4 garlic cloves, crushed and roughly chopped

4 fresh rosemary sprigs

3 tablespoons light olive oil

Salt and freshly ground black pepper

Preheat the oven to 140°C/275°F/Gas 1.

Trim the excess fat from the shoulder of lamb. Cut it into equal pieces, weighing about 200 g (8 oz) each. Combine the marinade ingredients in a bowl and add the lamb pieces. Rub the marinade into the lamb, cover and refrigerate for at least 6 hours, preferably overnight.

Remove the lamb from the marinade and season with salt and pepper. Heat the oil in a large flameproof casserole, until almost smoking, and fry the lamb pieces until well browned all over. Pour off any excess fat in the casserole and add the onion, carrot, celery and wine. Cover and cook in the oven for 1 hour.

Now remove the lid of the casserole and continue to cook in the same fashion, but turning the meat frequently, until the lamb is tender. The meat juices will reduce to produce a wonderful glaze on the meat.

Remove the lamb from the casserole and keep in a warm place. Add a splash of water to the cooking juices in the casserole and strain through a fine sieve into a bowl. Add the rosemary and whisk in the butter. Taste for seasoning and adjust if necessary.

To serve, simply divide the lamb between warm plates and spoon over a little sauce. Serve with new potatoes, if you wish.

ham shanks with horseradish cream, mushrooms and peas

This is the type of dish that will make you look like a true professional in the kitchen. The ham shanks can be prepared up to two days in advance, and the sauce is a great no-fuss winner.

Serves 6

3 ham shanks, weighing about 900 g (2 lb) each

FOR THE SAUCE

3 tablespoons unsalted butter

3 shallots or spring onions, finely chopped

175 g (6 oz) mushrooms, thinly sliced

Salt and freshly ground black pepper

2 tablespoons dry sherry

350 ml (12 fl oz) double cream

125 g (4½ oz) shelled peas

2–3 tablespoons creamed horseradish

Chopped fresh parsley, to garnish

Put the shanks in a large saucepan of cold water. Bring to the boil, simmer for 2 minutes, then refresh under cold water. Skim off any scum that rises to the surface, cover with a lid and simmer for 2½–3 hours or until the meat is very tender.

Transfer the shanks to a clean bowl and allow to cool. Reserve a little of the cooking liquid. When the shanks are cool enough to handle, remove and discard the skin. Flake the meat off the bone and cut into 2–3 cm (¾–1¼ in) chunks.

To make the sauce, melt the butter in a saucepan over a moderate heat and sweat the shallots or spring onions and mushrooms for 3 minutes with a little salt. Add the sherry and bring to the boil. Add the cream and peas and boil vigorously until the cream thickens.

To serve, warm the pieces of ham in a covered pan with a little of the cooking liquid (or in a microwave on full power for 3 minutes). Bring the sauce to the boil if necessary and add the creamed horseradish. Do not boil again or you will spoil the flavour of the horseradish. Season to taste with salt and pepper. Spoon the ham shanks into six warm bowls, cover generously with the sauce and sprinkle with the parsley.

If you prefer a fancier presentation, preheat the grill to medium-high. Gently stir 125 ml (4 fl oz) of whipped cream into the finished sauce, leaving it in large curds. Use this to cover the ham shanks, and glaze each plate under the hot grill for about 1 minute. Sprinkle with the parsley and serve at once.

braised pork perfumed with rosemary and juniper

This is a very gutsy, full-flavoured dish that has more than a hint of influence from the Continent. No vegetables are included in the recipe, but we would normally serve it with roast baby onions and mushrooms, and mash, pasta or soft polenta.

Serves 4–6

1 kg (2 lb 4 oz) shoulder of pork, cut into 75–100 g (3–4 oz) pieces (allowing 2 pieces per person)

Salt and freshly ground black pepper

50 g (2 oz) butter, plus 2 tablespoons butter, chilled

2 tablespoons light olive oil

1 large onion, finely chopped

6 garlic cloves, minced

3 tablespoons plain white flour

500 ml (18 fl oz) meat stock or 1 chicken stock cube and 500 ml (18 fl oz) water

1 tablespoon chopped fresh rosemary

2 tablespoons chopped fresh flatleaf parsley

1½ teaspoons juniper berries

Fresh rosemary sprigs, to garnish

FOR THE MARINADE

½ bottle of red wine

2 unpeeled garlic cloves, lightly crushed

1 tablespoon juniper berries, lightly crushed

2 fresh rosemary sprigs

A few parsley stalks

Place the pieces of pork in a stainless-steel or ceramic bowl. Add the marinade ingredients and toss. Cover and place in the fridge for 6 hours or preferably overnight.

To cook the pork, drain it first in a colander, reserving the marinade in a small saucepan. Discard any herbs that stick to the pork and pat the meat dry with a clean cloth. Season with salt and pepper.

Melt the 50 g (2 oz) butter and 1 tablespoon of the oil in a large, heavy saucepan or frying pan and brown the meat on all sides over a high heat. Take time to do this properly as the browning adds so much flavour and colour.

In another pan, fry the onion and garlic in the remaining oil until soft and light brown.

When the meat is brown, sprinkle it with the flour and allow to cook for about 5 minutes.

Meanwhile, bring the reserved marinade to a gentle simmer. You will see that it separates. Carefully strain the clear liquid onto the onion and discard the foamy residue.

Take the pork pan off the heat and add 125 ml (4 fl oz) of the stock, scraping at the bottom of the pan with a wooden spoon to release any caramelized bits or congealed flour. Now add the remaining stock, the onion and marinade, and ½ teaspoon salt. Bring to a very gentle simmer, then cover and cook slowly for 2 hours, until tender.

Add the chopped rosemary, parsley and juniper berries and swirl in the 2 tablespoons of butter. Garnish with sprigs of rosemary and serve.

pot-roasted guinea fowl with garlic and thyme

The key to this recipe is to use a decent, flameproof casserole with a tight-fitting lid. That way the guinea fowl roasts and steams at the same time, which ensures the meat is always kept moist.

Serves 4

10 garlic cloves
2 oven-ready guinea fowl
Salt and freshly ground pepper
4 fresh thyme sprigs
6 rashers of streaky bacon
2 tablespoons olive oil
50 g (2 oz) butter
250 ml (9 fl oz) Brown Chicken Stock (see page 232)
2 shallots, sliced
1 tablespoon chopped fresh thyme
Mashed potatoes, to serve

Blanch the garlic cloves in boiling water for 10 minutes. Refresh under cold water and drain.

Season the guinea fowl and put two garlic cloves and two thyme sprigs in the cavity of each. Cover each bird with three rashers of bacon and secure with string.

Heat the oil with 1 teaspoon of the butter in a large, flameproof casserole over a medium–high heat. Add the guinea fowl and cook on all sides, for about 5 minutes or until lightly browned. Lower the heat, cover the casserole with a tight-fitting lid, and cook for about 1 hour, turning the birds occasionally.

Add the stock, shallots and remaining garlic and cook for a further 15 minutes.

Remove the guinea fowl and rest on a warm plate for 10 minutes. Boil the stock for 5 minutes or until reduced by half. Remove the strings from the guinea fowl, then take off the breasts and legs. Keep aside in a warm place.

Chop the carcasses and add them to the reducing stock. Cook for another 15–20 minutes, allowing the stock to reduce a bit more. Strain into a clean bowl. Add chopped thyme and whisk in the remaining butter.

To serve, place a breast and a leg on each warm plate, along with some of the bacon. Pour the sauce over and around, and serve with mashed potatoes.

braised oxtail with red wine

Most people seem to be a bit afraid of oxtail, but Paul just loves its deep flavour. This tasty dish is perfect served with roast veg and some creamy mash or buttered noodles.

Serves 4

1.25 kg (2 lb 12 oz) large oxtails, cut into 5 cm (2 in) segments

Salt and freshly ground black pepper

3 tablespoons plain white flour

6 tablespoons light olive oil

140 g (5 oz) onions, roughly chopped

140 g (5 oz) carrots, roughly chopped

½ head of garlic, crushed

1 bottle of intense red wine, e.g. Rioja or Bordeaux

1 bouquet garni

1 tablespoon sugar

½ teaspoon cracked black peppercorns

2 tablespoons butter

Preheat the oven to 160°C/325°F/Gas 3.

Season the pieces of oxtail with salt and pepper and toss with the flour. Heat the oil in a heavy-based frying pan over a high heat, and brown the pieces of oxtail. As they brown, remove them to a braising dish that will fit in your oven.

When they are all browned, use the same pan, over a medium heat, to fry the onions, carrots and garlic until soft and lightly browned. Remove to the braising dish.

Pour off any fat from the pan and deglaze the pan with some of the red wine. Scrape the bottom of the pan with a wooden spoon to loosen all the delicious, caramelized juices. Add the rest of the wine and bring to the boil. Pour the liquid into the braising dish, add the bouquet garni and bring to a simmer on the hob. Cover tightly and place in the oven for 2½–3 hours. Check occasionally to see if there is enough liquid, and perhaps to turn the oxtail pieces.

When the oxtails are cooked, remove them from the sauce, with tongs or a slotted spoon and place on a serving dish. Cover and keep warm.

Strain the sauce through a sieve into a clean saucepan pressing down on the vegetables to extract as much of their juices as possible. Adjust the consistency of the sauce by adding water or a light stock if it is too thick, and reducing over a high heat if too thin. When you have the desired consistency, stir in the sugar, peppercorns and butter. Taste for seasoning, adding more salt or sugar as necessary.

Pour the sauce over the oxtails and serve with roast carrots and onions, and creamy mash or buttered noodles.

Nowadays it is common knowledge that vegetables are one of the best food categories health-wise as well as being generally low in both calories and fat. Vegetables are also packed with carbohydrates, fibre, vitamins and minerals. And, last but not least, they are very tasty items indeed.

We have to admit, however, that in the past, Ireland, like many parts of the United Kingdom, had a reputation for overcooked and underflavoured yuck when it came to vegetables. But that's certainly not the case any more. People now know that with quicker cooking times, not only the nutrients but also the flavour as well stay exactly where they belong – in the vegetable.

No longer are we limited to the basic old standbys: potatoes, cabbage, carrots and the humble swede. Just about any vegetable you can think of is now grown in Ireland, which means we are literally spoilt for choice.

Some vegetable dishes are complete and satisfying meals in themselves (as the increasing number of vegetarians will attest). Jeanne, in particular, would be totally content just with a big bowl of Champ or a plate of Carrot and Parsnip Mash (see pages 160 and 167). Filling, flavourful and full of goodness, what more could one ask for?

And everyone knows the Irish have an ongoing love affair with the potato. Since the days when it sustained the majority of the population, the humble spud has changed from a necessary item to a chosen one. Jeanne still can't get over how an Irish dinner table might offer up three to four different types of potato dishes: roast and mashed, boiled and gratined. Some Irishmen have been known to state proudly that they eat potatoes two or three times a day – amazing, but true.

We genuinely adore vegetables and their sheer diversity, and this chapter really is just the tip of the iceberg when it comes to Irish vegetables and their infinite possibilities.

vegetables and side dishes

champ

For us this is the ultimate Irish potato dish, although it is really a Northern Irish recipe. Paul's fondest memory of it is walking home from primary school at lunchtime to devour a large bowl of champ and a big glass of milk. He used to bury the butter in the champ and eat around it until at last it came bursting through the potato walls.

Serves 4

1 kg (2 lb 4 oz) floury potatoes, such as Kerr's Pink, King Edwards or Desiree

6 large spring onions

300 ml (½ pint) full-cream milk

4 tablespoons butter, plus extra to serve

Salt

Quarter the potatoes. Put them in a large saucepan of cold, salted water and bring to the boil. Simmer for 20–30 minutes until the potatoes are just cooked.

Pour off the water, cover the pan and let it sit in a warm place for about 3 minutes. This allows the potatoes to become soft and completely cooked.

While the potatoes are resting, wash and finely chop the spring onions. Combine the milk and 4 tablespoons butter in a small saucepan and bring to the boil. Put the chopped spring onions into the boiling milk, then remove from the heat and leave to infuse for about 1 minute. This mellows the raw onion taste.

Mash the potatoes and stir in the milk mixture until everything is smooth. Check for seasoning and add salt if necessary.

Serve on its own, in warm bowls, topped with a generous spoonful of butter.

colcannon cakes

Colcannon is to the south of Ireland what champ is to the north: a comfort food. Colcannon cakes are not quite so traditional, but they do work really well – providing your colcannon is not too sloppy or wet. We find we get a better result if we make the cakes with crushed new potatoes instead of the usual mashed floury type.

Makes 8 cakes

750 g (1 lb 10 oz) new potatoes, preferably the slightly waxy type, peeled and cut into 5 cm (2 in) cubes

85 g (3 oz) butter

About 1/3 Savoy cabbage, outer leaves removed, cored and finely chopped

1/2 bunch of spring onions, finely chopped

Plain white flour, for dusting

2 tablespoons light olive oil

Cook the potatoes in boiling salted water, then drain in a colander and set aside.

Heat 50 g (2 oz) of the butter with 150 ml (1/4 pint) of water in a medium-sized saucepan and add the cabbage. Cook over a high heat until the cabbage is just cooked, and the water has almost evaporated. Add the spring onions and cook until the mixture is just starting to fry.

Tip the cabbage into a bowl with the potatoes. Mash or crush the two together roughly (using your hands might work best). Shape the mixture into eight balls, dust with flour and press into neat patties.

Heat the oil with the remaining butter in a frying pan until the butter foams. Add the patties and cook over a medium heat for 3 minutes on each side. Drain on kitchen paper and serve at once.

creamy potato gratin

This is a very rich and delicious potato gratin. Leftovers make an absolutely stunning 'butty'. It is quite important that the potatoes are sliced evenly, for which you will probably need a mandolin.

Serves 4

500 g (1 lb 2 oz) potatoes, peeled and thinly sliced (no more than 3 mm/⅛ in thick)
Salt and freshly ground white pepper
A pinch of freshly grated nutmeg
1 garlic clove, finely chopped
1.2 litres (2 pints) whipping cream

Preheat the oven to 160°C/325°F/Gas 3.

Put the potato slices into a large bowl and season with salt and pepper and the freshly grated nutmeg. Rub the seasonings into the slices with your hands to ensure that they are evenly distributed. Mix the garlic with the cream, and mix this well with the potatoes.

Tip the mixture into an ovenproof gratin dish and pat it down. Cover with greaseproof paper and bake for 1 hour. You can remove the greaseproof paper and brown the gratin under the grill for about 2 minutes, until it is nice and golden brown, if you wish.

new potatoes with peas and ham

This is an ideal accompaniment to spring lamb. It is a simple dish that relies on top-class ingredients and a deft touch.

Serves 4

125 g (4½ oz) freshly shelled peas
50 g (2 oz) unsalted butter
A pinch of salt
85 g (3 oz) cooked ham, cut into matchsticks
250 g (9 oz) freshly cooked, hot new potatoes
1 tablespoon chopped fresh mint or parsley

Put the peas, 1 tablespoon of the butter, salt and 4 tablespoons of water into a medium-sized saucepan. Cover and cook vigorously for 3 minutes or until the peas are just cooked.

Add the ham, potatoes, mint or parsley and remaining butter. Shake the pan gently until the butter becomes creamy and sauce-like. Serve at once.

crusty sautéed potatoes

Everyone seems to love these sautéed potatoes. The secret is in the potato, which must
be a floury type to give the right texture. We use Kerr's Pinks, Maris Piper or King Edwards.
At the restaurant we cook up a large batch of spuds, then fry them as needed.

Serves 4

900 g (2 lb) floury potatoes, such as
Kerr's Pinks, Maris Piper or
King Edwards, unpeeled

1 tablespoon salt

6 tablespoons vegetable oil

3 tablespoons butter

FOR THE SPICED SALT

½ teaspoon salt

1 teaspoon garlic salt

1 teaspoon dried thyme

1 teaspoon paprika

Put the potatoes in a large saucepan with the salt and cover with cold water.
Bring to the boil, then simmer gently for 15–20 minutes until cooked. Drain and
allow to cool. Peel off the skins with a knife, and cut into slices about 1 cm
(½ in) thick.

Unless you have a huge frying pan, it is better to fry the potatoes in two
batches. Heat a pan over a high heat. Add half the oil and half the butter. When
the butter is foaming add half the potatoes and fry on each side until golden
and well crusted.

Mix together the spiced salt ingredients and season the potatoes with a little
of this mix.

Cook for a further minute, then drain on kitchen paper. If you are cooking in
batches, keep the first batch warm in the oven while you prepare the second
one, using the remaining oil and butter. Serve as soon as possible.

tobacco onions

One of our all-time-favourite vegetable accompaniments… good with almost everything!

Serves 4

4 large Spanish onions
1 teaspoon salt
Plain white flour, for dredging
Oil, for deep-frying

Cut the onions in half on the length, i.e. from the root to the point. Cut into thin slices against the grain. Place in a large bowl and sprinkle with the salt. With your hands, toss the onions, separating the pieces as you go. Allow to sit for 2–3 minutes. Toss the pieces in flour, pressing the flour into them to form a good crust.

Heat the oil to 180°C/350°F or until a cube of day-old bread turns brown in about 4–5 seconds. Deep-fry the onions until golden brown. Serve at once.

spiced cabbage

There are many ways to spice up the local Irish grub. This one was discovered by accident, but we find it works very well. Cabbage, like most of its relatives, does not keep very well when cooked so it is not a good idea to cook it too far in advance.

Serves 4

½ Savoy cabbage, outer leaves removed, cored and roughly chopped
4 tablespoons unsalted butter
2 teaspoons curry powder
Salt

Cook the cabbage in boiling, salted water for 3 minutes. Drain into a colander then refresh in cold water. Squeeze the cabbage to remove excess water.

Heat the butter in a large frying pan over a moderate heat until it foams. Add the cabbage, curry powder and a little salt. Fry for 3–4 minutes. Serve at once.

candied shallots

These simple little beauties seem to lift any roast meat to a higher realm.

Serves 4

24 shallots
40 g (1½ oz) butter
1 tablespoon vegetable oil
2 tablespoons sugar
200 ml (7 fl oz) red wine

Peel the shallots carefully, leaving the roots intact to keep them together. It is also nice to leave the wispy pointed ends on because they are so attractive.

Heat a large frying pan over a moderate heat. Add the butter and oil. When the butter is foaming, add the shallots and fry gently until they turn golden in colour. Add the sugar, and continue to cook for about 3 minutes until the sugar begins to caramelize. Add the wine, cover with a lid and cook gently for 10 minutes.

Remove the lid and boil off any excess liquid so that the shallots become beautifully glazed and candied.

cheesy yorkshire puddings

Paul likes to serve these with big chunks of meat, such as Beef Chop with Red Wine (see page 131) or even a simple sirloin steak. Jeanne thinks they are almost a meal in themselves.

Serves 4

175 g (6 oz) plain white flour
½ teaspoon salt
2 eggs
300 ml (½ pint) milk
115 g (4 oz) mushrooms, quartered
1 small aubergine, cut into
2 cm (¾ in) dice
2 tablespoons butter
6 tablespoons whipping cream
2 tablespoons grated Parmesan cheese
1 tablespoons chopped fresh parsley
Oil or beef dripping

Preheat the oven to 240°C/475°F/Gas 9.

In a medium-sized bowl, mix the flour and salt and make a well in the centre. Whisk the eggs and milk together, then whisk them into the flour to make a batter. Allow the batter to rest for at least 1 hour.

Sauté the mushrooms and aubergine separately in butter until they are light brown and tender.

Now combine the mushrooms and aubergine in a saucepan. Add the cream, Parmesan and parsley. Bring to the boil and take off the heat.

Pour the oil or beef dripping into bun tins or Yorkshire pudding moulds (using a tablespoon of oil per Yorkshire pudding) and heat in the oven until very hot. The fat should just be beginning to smoke. Quickly pour in the batter and cook for about 3 minutes, then add the cheesy mixture. Cooked in bun tins or Yorkshire pudding moulds these puddings will take about 6 minutes altogether.

tangy beetroot purée

A wonderful jazzy beetroot recipe that goes very well with goose, duck, pork or game.

Serves 4–6

350 g (12 oz) cooked beetroot, sliced
1 onion, finely chopped
1 garlic clove, crushed
3 tablespoons red wine vinegar
2 tomatoes, peeled, seeded and chopped
6 tablespoons stock or vegetable bouillon
1 teaspoon sugar
Salt and freshly ground black pepper

Preheat the oven to 180°C/350°F/Gas 4.

Place all the ingredients in an ovenproof dish and cover tightly with foil. Cook in the oven for 1 hour. Remove from the oven and purée in a food processor. Leave the purée a little chunky, or make it as smooth as you prefer. Check the seasoning and adjust to taste. Serve immediately.

carrot and parsnip mash

There is no definitive recipe for carrot and parsnip mash. It is simply some boiled carrots, some boiled parsnips and a good knob of butter, mashed together roughly. As you can imagine, some folks prefer more carrots than parsnips, some folk are the other way around. This is one of Jeanne's favourite things in the whole world (food-wise). She could eat two plates of this all by herself!

Serves 6–8

6 carrots, sliced
6 parsnips, sliced
3–4 tablespoons butter
Salt and freshly ground white pepper

Cook the carrots and parsnips separately in boiling, salted water until nicely tender but not too soft. Parsnips, in particular, have the ability to 'soak' up liquid, which could make it a mushy mash. Drain both vegetables well and mash them by hand or in a food processor, with the butter and salt and pepper. Check the seasoning and adjust if necessary.

This reheats really well in the microwave, so it can be one of those dishes you make in advance.

gratin of pumpkin

This gratin technique lends itself to most vegetables. At Christmas, we use it on the Brussels sprouts (without the sage) and everyone in the family loves it.

Serves 4–6

750 g (1 lb 10 oz) ripe pumpkin
25 g (1 oz) butter
Salt and freshly ground pepper
1 large garlic clove, halved
300 ml (½ pint) double cream
A pinch of freshly grated nutmeg
1 tablespoon chopped fresh parsley
½ tablespoon chopped fresh sage
2 tablespoons grated Parmesan cheese

Preheat the oven to 200°C/400°F/Gas 6.

Peel and seed the pumpkin. Cut it into 2 cm (¾ in) dice and sauté in a large frying pan with the butter and salt and pepper, until it is lightly golden. This will take about 5 minutes.

Sprinkle a small gratin or casserole dish with a little salt and rub the inside of the dish with the cut sides of the garlic. Tip the sautéed pumpkin into the dish.

Bring the cream to the boil and add a little salt and the nutmeg, parsley and sage. Pour this over the pumpkin and sprinkle with the Parmesan.

Bake in the oven for 10–15 minutes, until golden and luscious. Serve with game or lamb.

Great puddings are universally loved: they satisfy a sweet tooth and round out a fine meal. They remind people of childhood and the home. So, though they may not nourish the body, they do indeed nourish the soul.

Ireland has many of the same traditional nursery puds and sweets as the United Kingdom. Crème brûlées, bread-and-butter puddings, fruit crumbles and tarts are all long-established and time-honoured ways of using up surplus fruits and leftover baked goods. Apples and plums, rhubarb and berries have been grown for centuries all over the island, and the hedgerows and forests are usually abundant as well. Every housewife or housekeeper had a glut of traditional recipes for these scrumptious fruits handed down through the generations.

Jeanne did not grow up with any of these old favourites, and Paul would say it took a few years for her to get them spot on. However, once heading in the right direction, she became slightly obsessed with developing the best puddings around.

So here old standbys get new twists, like the Chocolate Bread-and-Butter Puddings with Marmalade Sauce or the Brown Bread Parfait with Bushmills Prunes (see pages 189 and 181). Then there are puddings that were just too good to be tampered with, such as the Bramley Apple Tart with a Walnut Crumble Topping or silky Blackberry Fools with Hazelnut Biscuits (see pages 195 and 170). Other recipes are more modern and light, like the Winter Fruit Soup with Sun-dried Cherries or the Fruit Gâteaux with Lemon Balm (see pages 179 and 202).

Most of the recipes featured here are quite simple and straightforward. They can also be made ahead of time and will keep well if there are actually any leftovers. So, what are you waiting for – give one a try.

puddings

blackberry fools with hazelnut biscuits

Remember the old saying 'the simple things are always the best'? With the simplicity of a fool and gorgeous fruit for free, everyone should try making this dish. The tasty biscuits keep very well in an airtight container.

Serves 4

300 g (10 oz) fresh blackberries

75–100 g (3–4 oz) caster sugar

Juice of 1 lemon

125 ml (4 fl oz) double cream

50 ml (2 fl oz) mascarpone cheese (optional, but if not used add an extra 50 ml/2 fl oz double cream)

FOR THE HAZELNUT BISCUITS

375 g (13 oz) caster sugar

250 g (9 oz) unsalted butter, softened

2 large eggs

1 teaspoon vanilla extract

280 g (10 oz) plain white flour

1 teaspoon bicarbonate of soda

1 teaspoon baking powder

140 g (5 oz) hazelnuts, roasted, skinned and chopped

Fresh sprigs of mint, to decorate (optional)

Reserve a few handfuls of blackberries and purée the remaining ones and the sugar in a food processor. Pass through a fine sieve. The resulting purée should be thick. The quantity of sugar relies heavily on the natural sweetness (or lack of it) of the blackberries. Add the lemon juice to the purée, then taste and adjust the flavouring if necessary.

Whisk the double cream until it just holds soft peaks, not any longer. Soften the mascarpone, if using, by beating by hand, then gently whisk the cream and mascarpone together. It is important not to over-beat the mixture or the fool will have a grainy texture. Lastly, fold the mixture with two-thirds of the purée.

Toss a few of the reserved blackberries in a spoonful of the remaining purée and place them in a wine glass. Fill the glass halfway with the creamy mixture. Place a thin layer of the purée on top of this, then fill the glass with more creamy mixture. Fill the other three glasses in the same manner. Chill in the fridge for at least 2 hours to firm the fools up.

Preheat the oven to 180°C/350°F/Gas 4.

To make the hazelnut biscuits, cream the sugar and butter together for 4 minutes. They should become light and fluffy. Add the eggs and vanilla and mix until they are all incorporated. Sift together the flour, soda and baking powder. Fold this into the butter/egg mixture by hand. Lastly, fold in the hazelnuts.

Using a spoon, drop spoonfuls onto a greased baking sheet, leaving space between them to allow for spreading. Bake in the oven for about 8 minutes, until golden brown. Remove from the baking sheet and cool on a wire rack.

Serve the fools with the hazelnut biscuits, and decorate each serving with a mint sprig, if you wish, and the reserved blackberries.

millefeuilles of tangy lemon curd and fresh strawberries

With or without the millefeuille pastry, this is a smashing sweet. Lemon and strawberries are simply glorious together, but this dish can be served with any other berry, so the strawberries could be changed to raspberries, blackberries or blueberries – just use whatever is ripe and at hand.

Serves 4

2 egg whites, lightly beaten

125 g (4½ oz) unsalted butter, melted

About 200 g (8 oz) good-quality filo pastry

75 g (2½ oz) caster sugar

About 450 g (1 lb) strawberries, hulled and halved or quartered

Icing sugar, for dusting (optional)

Freshly whipped cream, to serve

FOR THE LEMON CURD

1 egg

1 egg yolk

50 g (2 oz) sugar

Grated zest and juice of 1 lemon

50 g (2 oz) butter

125 ml (4 fl oz) whipping cream, whipped to soft peaks

First, cook the lemon curd. Simply place the egg, egg yolk and the sugar in a saucepan and whisk them together until the sugar has dissolved. Add the lemon juice and zest, and the butter. Whisk continually over a medium heat for about 5 minutes until the mixture has thickened. If you want to check with a thermometer, the curd is ready when it reaches about 160°C/325°F. Strain into a clean bowl and cover with clingfilm. When the curd has cooled completely, fold in the softly whipped cream and refrigerate.

Meanwhile, to prepare the filo pastry preheat the oven to 180°C/350°F/Gas 4. **Stir the egg** whites into the melted, but not hot, butter and mix well. Lay the sheets of filo out flat between sheets of clingfilm or greaseproof paper. A dampened tea towel laid over the top layer of the paper will help ensure that the filo does not dry out.

Taking one sheet of filo at a time, brush the melted butter/egg white mixture lightly all over the filo. Sprinkle generously with the caster sugar. Repeat this twice more, until three sheets of filo are pressed together. Cut this into rectangles about 10 cm (4 in) long by 4 cm (1½ in) wide (different brands of filo have differently sized sheets). You will want four of these rectangles for each portion. Arrange the rectangles on a baking tray and bake for about 7–10 minutes, until they are a nice glazed golden colour. Cool on a wire rack.

To serve, build the dessert by placing a filo rectangle in the centre of each plate. Gently place a spoonful of the tangy lemon curd on the rectangles, then carefully place a few strawberry pieces on this. Repeat until you have three layers. Dust the fourth rectangle liberally with icing sugar, if you wish, before placing it on top. Serve immediately, with freshly whipped cream.

pear crumble with a raspberry cream

Make sure you choose the right kind of pear for this, such as Comice, Conference or Concorde (a new cross-breed between the other two). If preferred, this recipe can be made with apples, for which crème chantilly (sweetened whipped cream), or even vanilla ice-cream would be a better accompaniment.

Serves 4

Juice of 1 lemon

6 ripe Comice, Conference or Concorde pears

About 4 tablespoons unsalted butter

4–8 tablespoons sugar, depending on pears

1 tablespoon plain white flour

Grated zest of 1 lemon

65 g (2½ oz) ground almonds

65 g (2½ oz) flaked almonds

FOR THE CRUMBLE TOPPING

50 g (2 oz) white sugar

50 g (2 oz) golden brown sugar

100 g (4 oz) plain white flour

100 g (4 oz) unsalted butter, chilled and diced

FOR THE RASPBERRY CREAM

200 g (8 oz) fresh or frozen raspberries

About 50 g (2 oz) sugar

1 teaspoon lemon juice

150 ml (¼ pint) whipping cream

Preheat the oven to 190°C/375°F/Gas 5.

To prepare the pears, place the lemon juice in a small bowl and, as you peel the pears, roll them in the juice to avoid discolouration. Halve the pears and scoop out the cores. Slice each half lengthways into about eight wedges. Return the pieces to the lemon juice.

Heat a large frying pan over a moderate heat and melt 2 tablespoons of the butter. When the butter has ceased foaming, add the pears and allow to cook for 3 minutes, shaking the pan gently as needed to prevent the pears from sticking. As necessary, add a little more butter. Sprinkle in the sugar and cook for a further 3–5 minutes; you may have to reduce the heat slightly. The pears should be quite soft and almost golden from the sweet buttery juices. Take off the heat and gently drain the slices of all excess liquid. Toss the slices with the flour and the lemon zest and set aside for the moment.

To prepare the crumble topping, mix together the sugars and flour and rub in the butter. When it is pea-consistency it is worked enough.

Sprinkle the ground almonds over the bottom of a shallow ovenproof dish. Lay the pear slices in next, to a depth of about 2.5 cm (1 in). Sprinkle the topping over the pears to a depth of about 1 cm (½ in). Scatter the flaked almonds over the top. Bake in the oven for about 30 minutes, until the top is golden and firm. Remove from the oven.

To make the raspberry cream, purée the raspberries in a food processor. Pass the purée through a sieve to remove the seeds. Add the sugar and lemon juice. Whip the cream until it just holds soft peaks and then fold it into the purée. Adjust the sweetness, if necessary, by adding a little more sugar.

To serve, scoop a big spoonful of the pear crumble into a soup plate or shallow bowl and top with a generous dollop of the raspberry cream. Serve at once, warm rather than hot.

toffee apples on sugar-glazed barmbrack

Barmbrack is the Irish equivalent of a yeasted fruit loaf. If you can't get your hands on any barmbrack, brioche would be a wonderful substitute, but a good-quality white loaf would be fine too.

Serves 6

1 loaf barmbrack (Irish fruit loaf) or brioche

100 g (4 oz) unsalted butter

50 g (2 oz) icing sugar

600 g (1 lb 5 oz) dessert apples, such as Granny Smiths or Cox's Orange Pippins

Juice of 1 lemon

140 g (5 oz) butter

100 g (4 oz) caster sugar

450 ml (16 fl oz) whipping cream

A few drops of vanilla essence

Preheat the grill to high.

To prepare the barmbrack, slice the loaf into twelve 2 cm (¾ in) thick slices. Either cut off the crusts and have neat rectangular shapes or leave the slices rather rustic. Spread each side with butter and evenly sprinkle on some of the icing sugar. Set aside.

Peel, core and halve the apples and cut each half into six wedges. Roll the wedges in the lemon juice to avoid discolouration.

Heat a large, heavy-based frying pan over a medium heat and add the butter. After it has foamed, toss in half the caster sugar and stir until it turns a nice medium-caramel colour. Toss in the apple wedges and cook over a medium-high heat until the wedges have a rich golden hue and can be pierced easily with a fork. This will take about 5 minutes.

Place the buttered and sugared slices of barmbrack on a baking sheet, put under the grill and watch closely. You just want an even golden toasting. Turn the slices over and glaze the other sides in the same manner.

Whip the cream until it holds fairly firm peaks and then fold in the remaining sugar and the vanilla essence.

To serve, place two glazed slices of barmbrack in the centre of each plate and carefully arrange the toffee apples on top. Add a dollop of the vanilla cream and serve immediately. For a really showy presentation you might want to add spun sugar on top of the apples.

baileys irish cream and white chocolate parfait with a warm chocolate sauce

The texture of this parfait is pure velvet, smooth and silky, with a to-die-for richness. With or without the warm chocolate sauce, this is a special sort of sweet, indulgent and… indulgent!

Serves 6–8

200 ml (7 fl oz) single cream
6 egg yolks
90 g (3½ oz) sugar
125 g (4½ oz) white chocolate, chopped and melted
200 ml (7 fl oz) double cream
½ tablespoon vanilla essence
3 tablespoons Baileys Irish Cream
Chocolate curls, to decorate (optional)

FOR THE WARM CHOCOLATE SAUCE
175 g (6 oz) good-quality dark chocolate
175 ml (6 fl oz) single cream
45 g (1½ oz) sugar

Place the single cream in a saucepan, bring just to the boil and set aside. Whisk the egg yolks and sugar together until the sugar has dissolved. Pour in the boiled single cream, stirring continuously. Return to the saucepan and cook over a medium heat, stirring constantly with a wooden spoon. Do not let it boil. The custard will be ready when the mixture coats the back of the spoon, or if a line drawn through the coating holds when the spoon is held up. It will take about 5 minutes to reach this stage. Strain the custard through a fine sieve into a mixing bowl, and stir in the melted chocolate. Using a food processor or hand-held electric whisk, beat at a medium-low speed for 5–10 minutes, until the chocolate mixture is cool.

Whisk the double cream until it holds soft peaks. When the chocolate mixture is cool fold in, by hand, the double cream, vanilla essence and Baileys Irish Cream. Pour the mixture into a 1.5-litre (2¾-pint) mould or ovenproof glass dish lined with clingfilm (or a terrine mould similarly lined) and cover with more clingfilm. Chill in the freezer for at least 4 hours, until set.

To make the warm chocolate sauce, melt the chocolate over a saucepan of hot, not boiling, water. Bring the cream to the boil in another saucepan and stir in the sugar to dissolve. Set aside until warm, not hot. Stir in the melted chocolate and whisk until smooth. Keep warm. The sauce will keep in the fridge for several days and can be reheated in a bain-marie or very carefully on medium heat in the microwave. Remember, though, once chocolate has been scalded the flavour is ruined.

To serve, either turn out the parfait and slice it, or spoon out two quenelles for each person. Place a slice of the parfait, or the quenelles, in the centre of each plate and drizzle the warm chocolate sauce over. To dress up the plate, sprinkle chocolate curls over the top.

pineapple crêpes suzette

It is really worth finding a Del Monte brand pineapple – their flavour is just so much better, every single time. These crêpes would also be delicious with banana, though in that case we would serve them with a Chocolate Sauce (see page 230).

Makes 12–16 crêpes, serves 4–6

125 g (4½ oz) plain white flour

50 g (2 oz) caster sugar

A pinch of salt

4 eggs

350 ml (12 fl oz) milk

1 teaspoon vanilla essence

50 g (2 oz) melted butter, plus 2–4 tablespoons melted butter, for cooking

Vanilla ice-cream or cream, to serve

FOR THE PINEAPPLE

1 ripe pineapple

60–100 g (2–4 oz) sugar

Juice of 1 orange

2 tablespoons lemon juice

2 tablespoons of Southern Comfort

A pinch of cracked black peppercorns and crushed mild chilli flakes (optional)

30–50 g (1–2 oz) butter

Make the crêpe batter at least 1 hour ahead of time, as it is necessary to let it rest. If you have a food processor you can simply process all the crêpe ingredients except the 2–4 tablespoons of melted butter and sieve them into a clean bowl. If you are making the crêpes manually, start with the flour, sugar and salt in a mixing bowl. Whisk in the eggs until smooth, then slowly stir in the milk, vanilla essence and the 50 g (2 oz) melted butter until the batter is smooth. Let it rest, covered with clingfilm.

To cook the crêpes, have one or two heavy-based (non-stick is preferable, but not necessary) frying pans, heating over a moderately high heat. Brush or rub the base of each pan with melted butter. When a drop of batter sizzles immediately, the pan is hot enough. Ladle about 3 tablespoons of batter into the pan, turning the pan quickly to coat the base evenly and thinly with the batter. Cook until the crêpe is light brown, about 1 minute, then turn it with a spatula, or toss it over, and let the other side cook. This will only take about half the time of the first side. Turn onto a plate or rack and make the remaining crêpes.

Peel and core the pineapple, then cut it into bite-size chunks, no bigger than 1 cm (½ in), trying to keep them about the same size to aid even cooking. Heat a frying pan over a moderately high heat and put some sugar in the dry pan. The amount will vary, depending on personal taste and the natural sweetness of the pineapple. When the sugar has dissolved and turned a rich golden caramel colour, add half the orange juice to stop the cooking process (or the caramel will burn). Toss in the pineapple chunks and sauté over a medium–high heat for about 3 minutes. The pineapple will release some of its natural juices, and will soften and become slightly transparent. Add another spoonful or two of the orange juice and the lemon juice, to taste, and deglaze with the Southern Comfort. Whether it flambés or not, the alcohol will burn off, leaving only the flavour and essence of the liqueur. (At this point, add a pinch of peppercorns and a pinch of chilli flakes if you wish.) Swirl in the butter and remove from the heat. Using a slotted spoon, remove the pineapple chunks to a warm dish.

Fold each crêpe in half and then half again, and return them to the pan, pressing them down until they are slightly heated, and are coated and soaked with all the juices. Put two crêpes on each plate, then arrange the pineapple chunks over and around the crêpes. Drizzle any remaining juices over. Serve at once. Vanilla ice-cream, or some cream, would go very well here.

pots of caramel cream with summer berries

The smooth, rich custard texture of this dish goes perfectly with summer berries just bursting with tangy flavour. It is equally delicious flavoured just with vanilla – to make it this way, use only 125 g (4½ oz) of sugar, adding it all at once to the eggs, and don't make the caramel.

Serves 4

250 ml (9 fl oz) milk
250 ml (9 fl oz) cream
1 vanilla pod, split
175 g (6 oz) sugar
1 egg
3 egg yolks
400 g (14 oz) summer berries, such as raspberries, strawberries, blueberries or blackberries
Fresh mint sprigs, to decorate
Icing sugar, sifted, to decorate

Preheat the oven to 150°C/300°F/Gas 2.

Place the milk, cream and vanilla pod in a large saucepan over a medium heat and bring to the boil. Set aside.

Place 125 g (4½ oz) of the sugar in a small, heavy-based saucepan with 2 tablespoons of water and cook over a medium heat. When the sugar has dissolved, let the liquid boil to a rich golden caramel colour. (A light caramel will become diluted in the custard and will not have a strong enough flavour). Remove from the heat and pour the caramel into the milk mixture. Return to a low heat to allow the caramel to melt back into the milk. When the milk has returned to the boil, it is ready.

Whisk the egg and the egg yolks and the remaining 50 g (2 oz) of sugar in a clean bowl until the sugar is dissolved. Slowly pour in the caramel milk, whisking continually. Strain through a sieve into another clean bowl; if there is a little froth on the top, carefully skim it off. Scrape the seeds out of the vanilla pod and put them back into the caramel milk.

Carefully pour the caramel milk mixture into four 150 ml (¼ pint) ramekins or bowls, and place them in a deep roasting tin. Pour enough boiling water into the tin to come up a third of the way up the sides of the ramekins and cover the whole bain-marie tightly with clingfilm. (Don't worry, the oven heat is too low to melt the clingfilm. Using foil sometimes discolours the custard.)

Place the tin in the centre of the oven and cook for 30–40 minutes. The centre of each custard should still wobble slightly as the custard will continue to cook even after it is removed from the oven. The low oven temperature is imperative to achieve the creaminess in the caramel creams.

Chill the ramekins in the fridge for a few hours, or overnight.

To serve, place a pile of summer berries on top of each caramel cream and scatter a few berries on the serving plate. Decorate with sprigs of mint and a dusting of icing sugar.

winter fruit soup with sun-dried cherries

For most people warm soups of custard and fruit may not spring to mind as a dessert option, but once you've tried one you'll be forever converted. Use good-quality fruit, canned or freshly poached. Sun-dried cherries are available in most supermarkets nowadays but, if you cannot find them, try sultanas or dried blueberries.

Serves 4

500 ml (18 fl oz) milk
½ vanilla pod, split
75 g (2½ oz) ground almonds
6 egg yolks
100 g (4 oz) caster sugar
50 ml (2 fl oz) Amaretto liqueur
4 poached pears, well drained
50 g (2 oz) sun-dried cherries, soaked in boiling water until cool, then drained
Amaretti biscuits, to serve (optional)
45 g (1½ oz) flaked almonds, toasted, to decorate

Place the milk, vanilla pod and ground almonds in a saucepan over a moderate heat and bring to the boil.

Whisk the egg yolks and sugar together in a bowl until the sugar is dissolved. Whisking continuously, slowly pour the milk into the yolk/sugar mixture and whisk together. Pour back into the saucepan and cook over a moderate heat, stirring continuously with a wooden spoon until the mixture has thickened enough to coat the back of the spoon. When it has reached the right thickness it will hold the line if you run your finger through the coating. Pass through a fine sieve, add the liqueur and transfer to a warm thermos flask to keep warm.

Halve and core the pears and cut them into fine slices.

To serve, arrange the pear slices and plumped-up cherries in soup plates and pour the warm custard sauce over and around them. Decorate with a sprinkle of toasted flaked almonds. Serve with an amaretti biscuit on the side, if you wish.

brown bread parfait with bushmills prunes

At first brown bread may sound like an unlikely ingredient for a parfait, but it really does work. The rich, nutty flavour of the soda comes through and blends well with the deep richness of the Bushmills whiskey.

Serves 4–6

85 g (3 oz) white chocolate, chopped

175 ml (6 fl oz) double cream

2 tablespoons milk

½ vanilla pod, split

3 egg yolks

1 tablespoon sugar

175 g (6 oz) brown soda bread, crusts removed and the bread broken up to make pea-size crumbs

2 tablespoons Bushmills Irish whiskey

Grated orange zest, to decorate (optional)

Icing sugar, sifted, to decorate (optional)

FOR THE BUSHMILLS PRUNES

50 ml (2 fl oz) orange juice

175 g (6 oz) sugar

½ orange

½ lemon

125 g (4½ oz) pitted prunes

4–6 tablespoons Bushmills Irish whiskey

To make the parfait, melt the white chocolate. Place half the cream, the milk and the vanilla pod in a small saucepan and bring to the boil.

Whisk the egg yolks and sugar together in a bowl until the sugar has dissolved. When the cream mixture has come to the boil, slowly pour it on to the yolk/sugar mixture, whisking continuously. Cook over a low heat until the custard is thick enough to coat the back of a spoon. When it has reached the right thickness it will hold the line if you run your finger through the coating. Strain through a fine sieve into a mixing bowl and allow to cool slightly.

Add the custard to the melted chocolate and fold in the breadcrumbs. Place in the fridge to chill for at least an hour.

Whip the remaining cream until it holds soft peaks and then fold it and the Bushmills into the custard and breadcrumbs mixture.

Pour into individual ramekins (about 100 ml/3½ fl oz capacity) and place in the freezer for at least 2–3 hours, or even overnight. Transfer from the freezer to the fridge for an hour or two before serving

To make the Bushmills prunes, place 175 ml (6 fl oz) of water, the orange juice, sugar and orange and lemon halves in a medium-sized saucepan and bring to the boil. Add the prunes, cover and simmer gently until soft, about 20 minutes. Take off the heat, remove the orange and lemon halves and add the Bushmills. Leave to cool.

To serve, dip each ramekin into hot water for a couple of seconds to loosen the parfait, then run a sharp knife around the edge. Carefully tip the parfait onto the centre of each plate and surround with the prunes and a little prune juice. Decorate with icing sugar and orange zest as desired, if you wish.

apple charlottes

This is one dessert that will never go out of fashion – it just has too much 'yummy'
factor. From the buttery crispy bread on the outside to the tender yet tart apple filling.
Serve with a Vanilla Custard Sauce (see page 231) or a Toffee Sauce (see page 230).
Some whipped cream or crème fraîche would round it out perfectly.

Serves 6

750 g (1 lb 10 oz) Bramley apples,
or a mixture of Bramley and Cox's

Juice and grated zest of 1 large lemon

250 g (9 oz) unsalted butter, softened

175 g (6 oz) caster sugar

12 slices of good-quality white bread,
such as a bloomer

Fresh sprigs of mint, to decorate (optional)

Icing sugar, sifted, to decorate (optional)

Vanilla Custard Sauce (see page 231)
or Toffee Sauce (see page 230),
to serve (optional)

Preheat the oven to 200º/400CºF/Gas 6. Grease four 175 g (6 oz) metal
pudding moulds.

Peel and roughly chop the apples, and sprinkle them liberally with the lemon
juice. Place all the apples in a heavy-based saucepan with a spoonful of the
butter. Add about 125 g (4½ oz) of the caster sugar, the remaining lemon juice
and the lemon zest (more sugar may be to your taste and can be added as you
desire. It also depends on the apples.) Cook over a medium-low heat, stirring
occasionally to prevent sticking, until the apples are soft and mushy. Do not use
a lid, as you want the cooking liquids to evaporate as much as possible. Don't
worry if there are some chunks; a bit of texture is nice.

Sprinkle about 3 tablespoons of the remaining sugar into the first pudding
mould and shake it until the entire inside of mould is well covered with sugar.
Pour the excess into the next mould and repeat the same process until you have
sugared all six moulds.

Remove the crusts from the slices of bread and brush both sides of the slices
with the softened butter. Cut the slices into strips about 4 cm (1½ in) wide and
slightly higher than the sides of the moulds. Cut six rounds, one for the base
of each mould. Place a round in each base and carefully line the sides of the
moulds with the strips. Overlap the strips slightly to ensure a complete covering
that will hold the apple filling

Fill each mould with the apple and, lastly, lay a round of buttered bread on the
top. (It does not matter if this doesn't fit perfectly as the top will be the bottom
when the charlotte is unmoulded).

Bake the charlottes in the oven for about 10 minutes, then reduce the
temperature to 160ºC/325ºF/Gas 3 and continue to cook for a further 20–30
minutes, until the bread is nicely golden brown and the charlottes are firm
enough to support themselves when they are unmoulded. Remove from the oven
and allow to cool slightly.

Turn the charlottes onto warm plates and decorate with sprigs of mint and
icing sugar, if you wish. Serve them with vanilla custard sauce, toffee sauce,
cream or crème fraîche as desired.

baked pears stuffed with almond and ginger

A simple filling of almond and ginger offers a complementary alliance of flavours for a good eating pear. Ideal for a buffet as the dish is so self-contained, the pears can be sliced and fanned in individual dishes before baking, and the filling sprinkled over them, for a different presentation.

Serves 4

Juice of ½ lemon

2 ripe pears, such as William, Conference, or Comice

4 teaspoons clear honey, to serve (optional)

100 g (4 oz) Greek-style yoghurt, to serve (optional)

Fresh sprigs of mint, to decorate (optional)

FOR THE ALMOND AND GINGER FILLING

75 g (2½ oz) almonds, skinned

75 g (2½ oz) ginger biscuits

50 g (2 oz) unsalted butter, at room temperature

25 g (1 oz) caster sugar

1 egg yolk

Preheat the oven to 190°C/375°F/Gas 5.

First make the filling. Toast the almonds until golden. Chop fairly finely. Crush the ginger biscuits roughly, using a rolling pin or the bottom of a clean, small saucepan. Mix the almonds, biscuits, butter, sugar and egg yolk until the ingredients hold together like a rough paste.

Place the lemon juice in a shallow dish. Peel the pears, rolling them in the lemon juice to prevent discolouration. Halve lengthways and core, (taking a little slice off the round side, to give a flat base for the half to stand on, is sometime necessary). Pack a round spoonful of the filling into each half. This should fill the cavity and cover most of the exposed half. Place the halves in an ovenproof dish and bake for 25–20 minutes, depending on the ripeness and type of pear used.

To serve, stir the honey into the Greek yoghurt, if using. Place two pear halves on each plate and scoop a dollop of the yoghurt beside them. Decorate with a sprig of mint, if you wish.

honey and ginger ice-cream with a plum compote

Nothing beats a home-made ice-cream, especially one made using good-quality ingredients. Fruit compotes provide an excellent accompaniment, but you can also serve them as a dessert in their own right with just a dollop of fresh cream.

Serves 6–8

500 ml (18 fl oz) milk
500 ml (18 fl oz) whipping cream
2 tablespoons peeled, chopped root ginger
1/2 vanilla pod
12 egg yolks
140 g (5 oz) caster sugar
100 ml (3 1/2 fl oz) clear honey
Chopped candied ginger
Fresh mint leaves, to decorate

FOR THE PLUM COMPOTE

900 g (2 lb) plums, stoned and halved
About 450 g (1 lb) sugar
1/2 vanilla pod
1/2 cinnamon stick
1 slice of orange

Put the milk, cream, ginger and vanilla pod in a saucepan, and bring to the boil. Remove from the heat and leave to infuse for 1 hour.

Whisk the egg yolks and sugar together until they are light and fluffy and the sugar is dissolved. Return the milk mixture to the boil and then, whisking continually, pour onto the yolk/sugar mixture. Return the mixture to the saucepan and, over a low heat, stir steadily and continually with a wooden spoon until it is thick enough to coat the back of the spoon. When it has reached the right thickness it will hold the line if you run your finger through the coating. Remove from the heat and strain through a fine sieve. Cool slightly and stir in the honey.

Prepare in an ice-cream machine according to the manufacturer's instructions. Alternatively, pour into a freezer container and freeze until firm, whisking every 30 minutes to break up the ice crystals.

The candied ginger can either be sprinkled into the ice-cream at the end of the freezing process or reserved to sprinkle over it when it is served.

To make the plum compote, first peel the plums, if desired, using the tip of a sharp knife. You can keep the plums halved, quartered, or even roughly chopped. Place all the ingredients in a large, heavy-based saucepan and place over a low to moderate heat. Taking care that the sugar does not burn on the bottom, cook the compote for 20 minutes, until the plums are soft but not so mushy that they are losing their shape. Remove from the heat and leave to cool.

Sometimes there is so much liquid released in the cooking of the plums that you may need to strain the excess off and reduce it, on its own, in a small saucepan, over a moderate heat. You may not want to return all the liquid to the plums, just enough to bring the liquid to your desired consistency.

Serve the ice-cream surrounded with the plum compote, decorated with mint leaves, and sprinkle over some candied ginger, if you wish.

irish autumn pudding

This is similar to a luscious summer pudding, but the gorgeous tartness of the Bramley apples adds another dimension to the usual very-berry pudding. The plums also work really well, adding great texture and colour.

Serves 6

400 g (14 oz) Bramley apples

400 g (14 oz) plums

250 g (9 oz) fresh or frozen blackberries

125 g (4½ oz) golden brown sugar

125 g (4½ oz) dry red wine

4 tablespoons crème de cassis (blackcurrant liqueur)

About 10–12 slices of white bread, crusts removed

Fresh mint sprig, to decorate (optional)

A sprig of redcurrants, to decorate (optional)

Cream or crème fraîche, to serve

FOR THE BERRY SAUCE

450 g (1 lb) fresh or frozen blackberries or mixed berries

Juice of 1 lemon, or to taste

140 g (5 oz) sugar, or to taste

Peel, core and roughly chop the apples. Aim to make the pieces about the same-size so that they cook evenly.

Halve and stone the plums and roughly chop them. Place the apples and plums in a medium-sized saucepan along with the blackberries, sugar and wine and place over a medium heat. Bring to the boil then simmer gently for about 15 minutes, or until the apple pieces are soft and rather mushy.

Take off the heat and add the crème de cassis. Leave to cool.

Line the inside and base of a 1-litre (1¾-pint) bowl or mould with the slices of bread. Overlap the slices slightly on the sides to ensure that the filling does not leak through. Any leftover bits of bread can be used to cover the filling (this will be the bottom of the pudding when it is turned out).

Place the cooked, cooled fruit carefully in the lined mould and press it down quite firmly. Fill it nearly to the top, then cover it completely with the remaining bread. Weigh this down with a can on a plate and place in the fridge overnight.

To make the berry sauce, simply purée the berries with the lemon juice and sugar in a food processor. Pass through a fine sieve and taste for flavour. Adjust with more sugar or lemon juice as necessary.

To serve, carefully turn the pudding out onto a serving plate. Brush any uncoloured bits of bread with a little sauce and decorate with a mint sprig and a sprig of redcurrants on the top, if you wish. Cut the pudding into wedges and serve with a dollop of fresh cream or crème fraîche, and some of the berry sauce on the side.

fruit loaf bread-and-butter puddings

We find this interpretation far more interesting than many of the other fruit loaf recipes we've tried, and infusing the custard base with orange really helps to bring out the fruit flavours. Making the dough in a food processor is quicker and far easier than by hand.

Serves 8

Vegetable oil, for greasing
1 teaspoon fresh yeast
3 tablespoons warm milk
375 g (13 oz) plain white flour
1 teaspoon salt
25 g (1 oz) sugar
4 eggs
300 g (10 oz) unsalted butter, at room temperature
25 g (1 oz) glace cherries, finely chopped
50 g (2 oz) raisins or sultanas
25 g (1 oz) chopped peel, finely chopped

FOR THE BREAD-AND-BUTTER PUDDINGS
500 ml (18 fl oz) milk
500 ml (18 fl oz) whipping cream
1 teaspoon vanilla essence
1/2 orange
250 g (9 oz) sugar
4 eggs
6 egg yolks

Grease a 450 g (1 lb) loaf tin. Dissolve the yeast in the warm milk and leave in a warm place for about 10 minutes, until frothy. Place the flour, salt, sugar and eggs in a mixing bowl. Add the yeast mixture and mix by hand until the dough is coming together. Slowly, little by little, add the butter, letting the dough incorporate it each time. The dough should turn shiny, elastic and be quite soft. Alternatively, if you have a food processor with a dough-hook attachment we'd recommend that you use it to mix the dough together (on medium speed for about 3 minutes), as it will really save you time. Lastly, toss in the dried fruits and peel. Turn into a greased bowl and cover with clingfilm. Leave to rise in a warm place until doubled in size, about 1 hour.

When the dough has risen, turn it out onto a work surface and shape it to fit into the prepared loaf tin. Cover with clingfilm and again leave the dough to rise until it doubles in size. This time it should not take as long, about 40 minutes.

Preheat the oven to 190°C/375°F/Gas 5. Bake the loaf in the centre of the oven for about 45 minutes. It should sound hollow when tapped on the bottom. Cool on a wire rack. The loaf will freeze very well if wrapped tightly in clingfilm.

For the pudding, put the milk, cream, vanilla and orange in a saucepan over a heat and bring to the boil. Set aside and leave to infuse for about 20 minutes.

Whisk the sugar, eggs and egg yolks together until the sugar has dissolved and the mixture is light and fluffy. Strain in the cream/milk mixture, whisking continually. Strain again through a fine sieve. Set aside.

Reduce the oven temperature to 150°C/300°F/Gas 2.

Slice eight 5 mm (1/4 in) slices of fruit loaf. Cut off the crusts and dry them out, either in the oven or by toasting them lightly in a toaster. Arrange a slice in each of eight small ovenproof bowls and gently pour in the pudding mixture until the bowls are nearly full. Place the bowls in a bain-marie one-third full of boiling water, and cover the whole bain-marie with clingfilm. (The oven is not hot enough to melt the clingfilm.) The clingfilm will prevent a crust from forming on the puddings and will also help to distribute the heat more evenly. Bake in the oven until the puddings are just set (the centres will still be wobbly). Remove from the oven and remove the clingfilm. Leave to cool in the bain-marie.

Some people prefer their pudding still warm, others slightly chilled.

chocolate bread-and-butter puddings with marmalade sauce

Chocolate adds another dimension to this old favourite. If preferred, one large ovenproof dish can be used instead of individual bowls.

Serves 6

500 ml (18 fl oz) milk

500 ml (18 fl oz) single cream

Grated zest of 1 orange

1 vanilla pod, split

100 g (4 oz) cocoa

1/2 loaf unsliced white bread

8 egg yolks

2 eggs

100 g (4 oz) caster sugar

200 g (8 oz) dark chocolate, melted

350 g (12 oz) chunky marmalade, for the marmalade sauce

Icing sugar, sifted, to decorate (optional)

Fresh mint sprigs, to decorate (optional)

Place the milk, cream, orange zest and vanilla pod in a saucepan and bring to the boil. Remove from the heat, whisk in the cocoa, and leave to infuse for about 30 minutes.

Preheat the oven to 150°C/300°F/Gas 2.

Remove the crusts from the bread and cut it into six 5 mm (¼ in) slices. Cut each slice on the diagonal and place two triangles of bread in 6–8 ramekins.

Whisk together the egg yolks, eggs and sugar until the sugar has dissolved. Strain the milk and cream mixture through a fine sieve onto the eggs and sugar and whisk together. Finally, add the melted chocolate and stir well.

Ladle the mixture gently into 6 small ramekins so as not to disturb the bread. Place the ramekins in a deep roasting tin. Pour in enough boiling water to come a third of the way up the sides of the ramekins. Cover the bain-marie with clingfilm and place it in the oven for about 40–50 minutes. (The oven is not hot enough to melt the clingfilm.) The centres of the puddings should just shake slightly when they are ready.

Remove the puddings from the oven, and remove them from the bain-marie.

To make the marmalade sauce, place the marmalade and 250 ml (9 fl oz) of water in a small saucepan and bring slowly to the boil. Stir and remove from the heat.

To serve, cover the top of each pudding with a spoonful of the sauce. Alternatively, serve the sauce on the side, add a mint sprig and simply sprinkle a little icing sugar onto each pudding for decoration.

sticky toffee puddings with a bushmills butterscotch sauce

An all-time favourite, this sticky toffee pudding gets real depth of flavour from the intense sweetness of the dates. The generous dose of Bushmills Irish whiskey cuts through the butterscotch sauce with great character.

Serves 6–8

200 g (8 oz) fresh dates, stoned and finely chopped
175 g (6 oz) self-raising flour
1 teaspoon bicarbonate of soda
1 teaspoon vanilla essence
1 tablespoon coffee essence
100 ml (3½ fl oz) milk
85 g (3 oz) unsalted butter
140 g (5 oz) sugar
2 eggs, beaten just to break the yolks
Vegetable oil, for greasing
Whipped cream, to serve

FOR THE BUTTERSCOTCH SAUCE
3 tablespoons unsalted butter
8 tablespoons golden brown sugar
200 ml (7 fl oz) whipping cream
200 ml (7 fl oz) Bushmills Irish whiskey
1 tablespoon vanilla essence

Preheat the oven to 180°C/350°F/Gas 4.

Pour 175 ml (6 fl oz) of boiling water over the dates and set aside to soak and cool. Sift the flour and soda together. Add the essences to the milk. Cream the butter and sugar together until light and fluffy. Add the eggs slowly, waiting until each addition has been incorporated each time, before adding more.

Fold the flour and milk alternately into the egg mixture. Lastly, pour in the dates. The mix will be rather light and runnier than a cake batter. Ladle into 6–8 greased individual moulds and place on a baking sheet in the centre of the oven. Bake for about 30 minutes, until the puddings are firm and starting to pull away from the sides of the moulds. Remove from the oven and turn out onto a wire rack to cool.

To make the butterscotch sauce, put the butter in a medium-sized saucepan over a medium-high heat. When the butter is bubbling, add the sugar. Stir together for about 3 minutes, until the sugar has dissolved, and the whole mass is foaming, and bubbling. Carefully pour in the cream, followed by the Bushmills, and turn down the heat. Let it all come together and boil for about another minute or two, and then remove from the heat. Add the vanilla. Allow to cool slightly.

To serve, place the puddings on warm plates and ladle a generous spoonful of the sauce over each one. Dollops of whipped cream will top them off perfectly.

If wrapped in clingfilm, the puddings keep well for a couple of days, and can be reheated in just a minute or two in the microwave or covered in some of the sauce in a medium oven.

dark chocolate pudding soufflés with a baileys irish cream milkshake sauce

Just the thought of hot, soft soufflé with a cold, creamy milkshake sauce is enough to tempt you to try this pudding. And the flavours are wonderfully concentrated.

Serves 4–6

Unsalted butter, softened
85 g (3 oz) caster sugar
75 g (2½ oz) golden brown sugar
4 eggs, separated
125 ml (4 fl oz) whipping cream
4 egg whites
50 g (2 oz) sugar
350 g (12 oz) Mi Amer or other good-quality dark chocolate, melted
50 ml (2 fl oz) Irish whiskey

FOR THE MILKSHAKE SAUCE
600 ml (1 pint) good-quality milk chocolate ice-cream
150 ml (¼ pint) Baileys Irish Cream

Preheat the oven to 190°/375°F/Gas 5.

To prepare the soufflé dishes liberally butter 4–6 small dishes and then sprinkle caster sugar into one of them. Rotate the dish until it is coated in sugar and tip any excess into the next dish. Continue until all the dishes are coated.

To make the soufflés, whisk together the golden brown sugar, egg yolks and two of the egg whites. Whisk continually over a saucepan of simmering water until the mixture has doubled in volume and is at the ribbon stage and hot to the fingertip.

Using a food processor or hand-held electric whisk, whisk on high for about 5–7 minutes until the mixture has almost completely cooled, and has quadrupled in volume.

Whip the cream just until it holds soft peaks, and leave to warm up to almost room temperature. (It is important to try to have all the ingredients close in temperature as this will ensure homogenous mixing.)

Whisk the remaining six egg whites until stiff and glossy with the 50 g (2 oz) sugar. Set aside.

Add the melted chocolate to the egg/sugar mixture and then fold in the whipped cream. Lastly, fold in the whiskey and then the egg whites.

Carefully place the soufflé mixture in the moulds, filling them about three-quarters full. If cooking immediately, the soufflés will take 15–18 minutes to cook. If they are being refrigerated for some time, you may need to add a few minutes to the cooking time to ensure that they are cooked right through.

While they are cooking, simply blitz the ice-cream and Baileys Irish Cream in a food processor. The sauce should be thick and frothy, and very cold.

Serve the soufflés immediately with the milkshake sauce on the side.

deep-dish sour cream and apple pie

Everyone loves apple pie. It is one of those humble, comforting desserts that is always welcome, especially on chilly evenings.

Serves 4

450 g (1 lb) Sweet Shortcrust Pastry (see page 235)

1 kg (2 lb 4 oz) Cox's Orange Pippins or other tasty dessert apples

Juice of 2 lemons

Grated zest of 1 lemon

500 ml (18 fl oz) soured cream

2 large eggs

350 g (12 oz) caster sugar

1 tablespoon vanilla essence

75 g (2½ oz) plain white flour

2 teaspoons ground cinnamon

Butter, for greasing

2 egg yolks, beaten

Crème fraîche, whipped cream or cinnamon ice-cream, to serve

Roll out the pastry to 3 mm (⅛ in) thick and cut it into two rounds, one with about a 25 cm (10 in) diameter, and the other with a diameter of 28–30 cm (11–12 in). Chill for 30 minutes.

Peel and finely slice the apples, tossing the slices in the lemon juice. Set aside. Put the lemon zest, cream eggs, sugar, vanilla, flour and cinnamon in a separate bowl and stir until smooth and homogenous.

Grease a slope-sided pie dish and line it with the smaller round of pastry. Chill again for 30 minutes.

Preheat the oven to 180°C/350°F/Gas 4.

Brush the base of the pie with egg yolk. This helps to seal the pastry, preventing it getting too soggy from the filling during baking.

Toss the apples with the cream/egg mixture and pile into the base, heaping the filling into a generous dome. The cream/egg mixture will set as it cooks, so when you pour it in make sure that it doesn't flow over the perimeter of the base.

Take the second pastry round from the fridge. Brush the perimeter of the base with egg yolk, then gently position the top piece and seal the edges of the pastry rounds. Trim the edges so that a sealed margin of about 2 cm (¾ in) of pastry is left. This can be pinched into a decorative shape with your thumb and forefinger. With a knife tip, slit the lid in a few places to allow steam to escape during cooking, and brush the lid with egg yolk. It will turn a nice shiny golden as it bakes.

Bake in the oven for approximately 45–55 minutes. The pastry should be firm and golden, and the apple slices should pierce easily with a skewer.

Remove from the oven and leave to cool. Serve with a big scoop of crème fraîche, whipped cream or cinnamon ice-cream.

bramley apple tart with a walnut crumble topping

The Bramley is considered by many to be the world's best cooking apple. Its natural tartness, when cooked, is the perfect foil for a sugary topping such as this crumble.

Serves 4

250 g (9 oz) Sweet Shortcrust Pastry (see page 235)

1 egg yolk, mixed with 1 tablespoon water

FOR THE FILLING

8–10 Bramley apples, weighing about 500 g (1 lb 2 oz) in total

Juice and grated zest of 1 lemon

100 g (4 oz) sugar

2 teaspoons ground cinnamon

50 g (2 oz) unsalted butter

2 tablespoons cornflour

FOR THE CRUMBLE

75 g (2½ oz) granulated sugar

75 g (2½ oz) soft brown sugar

45 g (1½ oz) plain white flour

1 teaspoon ground cinnamon

75 g (2½ oz) walnuts, toasted, peeled and chopped

50 g (2 oz) unsalted butter, chilled and diced

Grease a medium-sized tart tin with a little butter. Line the prepared tin with the pastry, rolled to a thickness of about 3 mm (⅛ in). Chill for 30 minutes. Preheat the oven to 190°C/375°F/Gas 5.

Cover the pastry with greaseproof paper and fill with baking beans. Bake blind (see page 235) in the oven for about 20 minutes, until nice and golden.

Remove the paper and beans. Brush the base and sides of the pastry case with egg yolk and water wash. This seals the pastry from the filling, thus preventing a soggy crust. Peel, core and roughly chop the apples. Toss them in the lemon juice. Sprinkle over the lemon zest, sugar and cinnamon and mix them in.

Melt the butter in a large saucepan, over a moderate heat and add the apples Cook, stirring frequently, until the apples turn to mush. Continue to cook, stirring frequently so that the apples don't stick, until almost all the juices have evaporated and the filling is fairly dry. Stir in the cornflour. You may need to add more sugar, depending on your individual taste and, of course, how tart the apples are – but remember, the crumble topping will add lots of sweetness.

Place all the crumble ingredients in a food processor and process until they are a pea-size consistency. Be very careful not to over-process, or the butter will start to melt and the topping will become one big, heavy mass. Store in the fridge until needed.

Increase the oven temperature to 200°C/400°F/Gas 6.

To assemble, put a generous amount of filling into the pastry case, taking care not to let it reach the top of the case. Sprinkle lots of the topping over the apple filling, again keeping well clear of the top of the case. Bake for about 15 minutes, until the topping is golden and crisp. Remove from the oven.

Slice into wedges when the tart is just warm, and serve with a large dollop of whipped cream or even crème fraîche.

pear and chocolate almond cream tart

It is amazing how well pears and chocolate go together. They really 'work'. The almond cream can be made without chocolate, and would then marry well with apricots, peaches or even cherries.

Serves 4–6

Butter, for greasing

250 g (9 oz) Sweet Shortcrust Pastry (see page 235)

1 egg yolk, lightly beaten

125 g (4½ oz) unsalted butter

125 g (4½ oz) caster sugar

About 1 teaspoon plain white flour

125 g (4½ oz) ground almonds

2 eggs, lightly beaten

100 g (4 oz) dark chocolate, melted

4–6 poached pears, drained and sliced into fans

25 g (1 oz) sliced almonds, toasted

3 tablespoons apricot jam and 3 tablespoons Sugar Syrup (see page 231), for the glaze (optional)

Chocolate Sauce (see page 230), to serve (optional)

Grease a 23–25 cm (9–10 in) fluted flan tin with a little butter.

Roll the pastry to about 5 mm (¼ in) thick and use it to line the tin. Chill in the fridge for at least 30 minutes.

Preheat the oven to 180°C/350°F/Gas 4.

Cover the pastry with greaseproof paper and fill with baking beans. Bake blind (see page 235) in the oven for about 10 minutes until golden. Remove the paper and beans and brush the inside of the pastry case lightly with the egg yolk to seal the pastry and prevent it becoming soggy.

Reduce the oven temperature to 160°C/325°F/Gas 3.

Cream together the butter and sugar. Add the flour and then the ground almonds. Mix well. Slowly add the eggs and finally pour in the melted chocolate. This chocolate almond cream can be stored in an airtight container in the fridge for several days.

Using a piping bag without a nozzle (or a palette knife) evenly distribute the cream over the base of the pastry case to a depth of no more than 2 mm (¹⁄₁₆ in).

Fan the pear slices on top of the cream, pressing gently into the cream. Sprinkle the sliced almonds generously over the top and place the tart on a baking tray. Bake in the oven for about 30–45 minutes. It's important that the chocolate almond cream is completely cooked. A toothpick inserted into the centre should come out clean. Remove the tart from the oven and leave to cool.

A light glaze will improve the tart's appearance. Melt the glaze ingredients in a small saucepan and, when they have come to the boil, use a pastry brush to lightly coat the top of the tart.

This dish is perfect served with chocolate sauce.

lemon-scented cheese and berry tartlets

The light lemon and cheese mixture is creamy and tangy and balances perfectly with the sweet berries used here. Always choose ripe, unbruised berries; whatever is in season will always taste best.

Serves 4

Butter, for greasing

250 g (9 oz) Sweet Shortcrust Pastry (see page 235)

1 egg yolk, lightly beaten

400 g (14 oz) berries, such as raspberries, blackberries, strawberries or blackcurrants

Whipped cream and/or Berry Sauce (see page 186), to serve

Icing sugar, sifted, to decorate

FOR THE FILLING

225 g (8 oz) full-fat cream cheese

150 ml (¼ pint) soured cream

1 egg

75 g (2½ oz) caster sugar, or to taste

¾ teaspoon vanilla essence

Grated zest and juice of ½ lemon, or to taste

Preheat the oven to 180°C/350°F/Gas 4. Lightly grease four 10 cm (4 in) tartlet tins with a little butter. Roll out the pastry to just 3 mm (⅛ in) thickness and line the tartlet tins. Chill in the fridge for at least 20 minutes.

Cover the pastry in each tin with greaseproof paper, fill with baking beans and bake blind (see page 235) to a golden brown, about 10 minutes. Remove the paper and beans. Brush the insides of the tartlet cases lightly with the egg yolk, to prevent the pastry becoming soggy. Set aside to cool.

Reduce the oven temperature to 150°C/300°F/Gas 2.

To prepare the filling, whisk all the ingredients together, either in a mixer or by hand, until the mixture is smooth and homogenous. Taste for flavour. Depending on the lemon, you may want to add slightly more lemon juice or slightly more sugar. You want the filling to be nice and tart to balance the natural sweetness of the berries.

Spoon the filling into the tartlet cases, taking care not to spill any over the edges, and bake in the oven for just 8 minutes. The centres of the tartlets should be wobbly when you remove them from the oven. They will continue to cook even after being removed. Leave to cool.

When the tartlets are cool, remove them from the tins. Arrange a generous pile of berries on top of each tartlet. A sprinkle of icing sugar over the berries adds an attractive finish. The tartlets can be served with a dollop of whipped cream, or a berry sauce or both.

chocolate roulade with fresh raspberries

This dessert is like a Swiss roll – but the richness of the chocolate sponge and the fresh delicate flavour of the raspberries elevates it to the winners' circle. Everyone will return for seconds, so be prepared. You can serve the roulade with extra raspberry sauce on the side if you like.

Serves 6–8

Butter, for greasing

6 eggs, separated, at room temperature

250 g (9 oz) icing sugar, sifted

25 g (1 oz) cornflour

100 g (4 oz) good-quality cocoa

350 ml (12 fl oz) whipping cream

50 g (2 oz) caster sugar

1 teaspoon vanilla essence

100 ml (3½ fl oz) good-quality raspberry jam

225 g (8 oz) fresh raspberries, picked over

Raspberry sauce, made as per Berry Sauce (see page 186), to serve (optional)

Raspberries, to decorate

Fresh mint leaves, to decorate

Preheat the oven to 190°C/375°F/Gas 5. Grease a baking tray measuring about 30 x 40 cm (12 x 16 in) with a little butter and line it with baking parchment.

Using a handheld electric mixer whisk together the egg yolks and 175 g (6 oz) of the icing sugar on high for about 3 minutes, until very pale and fluffy. Set aside.

In a clean bowl, whisk the egg whites until they hold soft peaks. Slowly add the remaining icing sugar and continue to whisk until the whites are shiny, glossy and firm.

Sift the cornflour and cocoa together. Fold this into the egg-yolk mixture alternately with the egg whites. The mixture needs to be well blended. Spread the mixture evenly on the prepared baking tray and bake in the oven for 8 minutes.

Meanwhile, whip the cream until it holds soft-peaks, so it must not be too firm. Fold in the caster sugar and vanilla and set aside. The cream should be quite firm now.

Blend the jam with 2 tablespoons of water and set aside.

Put a clean tea towel on your work surface and cover it with a large sheet of greaseproof paper.

When the sponge is cooked, remove it from the oven. Release it from the sides of the baking tray by running a sharp knife around the edges, and then turn it out onto the greaseproof paper. If there are any crusty bits along the edges it is a good idea to trim them, as they can hamper the rolling process.

While the sponge is cooling, brush on the diluted jam mixture, covering its whole surface. Next, spread on a layer of the flavoured whipped cream, leaving a border of about 5–6 cm (2–2½ in) at each of the lengthways sides of the sponge. This layer of cream should be about 2 cm (¾ in) thick.

Gently sprinkle on a generous layer of raspberries. You're aiming for a raspberry in every bite, so plenty of them need to be spread across the cream layer.

Starting at the side furthest from you, roll the sponge up lengthways, curling it over on itself with the help of the greaseproof paper. Make sure the top edge is tucked under before rolling too far. Don't press too hard or the cream will squish out of the sides. Finish with the seam of the cake underneath the roulade.

Transfer the roulade to a clean tray or baking sheet and use a clean tea towel to correct the shape, if need be. Jeanne always tucks it firmly around the roulade, ensuring an even cylinder shape. Chill in the fridge for at least an hour.

To serve, simply cut slices about 2 cm (¾ in) thick at an angle, and lay in the centre of each plate. Decorate with a few fresh raspberries and a mint leaf. Serve with raspberry sauce, if you wish.

lemon tart

This tart is one of Paul's favourite desserts when made properly. The tartness, which could just as easily come from limes or even passion fruit, keeps the creamy filling tangy rather than cloying. All it needs is a dollop of whipped cream.

Serves 6–8

Butter, for greasing
250 g (9 oz) Sweet Shortcrust Pastry (see page 235)
8 eggs
350 g (12 oz) caster sugar
Grated zest of 4 lemons
250 ml (9 fl oz) whipping cream
Juice of 10–12 lemons
1 egg yolk, lightly beaten
Whipped cream, to serve

Grease a **23–25 cm** (9–10 in) flan ring with a little butter. Roll out the pastry to 3 mm (⅛ in) thickness and line the prepared ring. Place in the fridge to chill for 30 minutes.

Preheat the oven to 180°C/350°F/Gas 4.

Whisk the eggs, sugar and lemon zest until the mixture is light in colour and trails off the whisk in ribbons. Slowly whisk in the cream. Add three-quarters of the lemon juice, then taste, and add the remaining juice if needed. Set aside.

Cover the pastry with greaseproof paper and fill with baking beans. Bake blind (see page 235) in the oven for about 15–20 minutes. Remove the paper and beans and brush the case with the egg yolk to seal the pastry and prevent the filling from leaking.

Reduce the oven temperature to 160°C/325°F/Gas 3.

Fill the pastry case with the lemon filling to just below the rim of the pastry. Bake for 25–30 minutes, until only the centre of the tart wobbles slightly. The filling will continue to cook when removed from the oven. Leave to cool.

To serve, cut into wedges and serve with whipped cream.

pear and walnut upsidedown cake

Upsidedown cakes are a traditional favourite in the United States. You can use canned pineapple, but we prefer fresh fruit as the flavours seem to merge more. A Toffee Sauce (see page 230) is great served with this cake, as is the usual dollop of whipped cream.

Serves 6–8

175 g (5½ oz) butter, for greasing

45 g (1½ oz) caster sugar

45 g (1½ oz) light brown sugar

2–3 ripe pears

25 g (1 oz) walnut halves, skinned and lightly roasted

Whipped cream and/or Toffee Sauce (see page 230) or caramel sauce, to serve

FOR THE SPONGE BATTER

45 g (1½ oz) unsalted butter

75 g (2½ oz) caster sugar

50 g (2 oz) plain white flour

2 teaspoons baking powder

½ teaspoon bicarbonate of soda

A pinch of salt

½ teaspoon ground cinnamon

¼ teaspoon ground cloves

¼ teaspoon ground nutmeg

1 egg

60 ml (2¼ fl oz) buttermilk

Preheat the oven to 180°C/350°F/Gas 4. Grease a 23 cm (9 in) round or square cake tin with a little melted butter.

Pour the melted butter into the cake tin. Add the caster sugar and light brown sugar and stir together until the sugars are mixed in with the butter.

Peel, halve and core the pears. Arrange them attractively, curved-side down, in the butter/sugar mix. Place the walnut halves between each pear half.

To make the sponge batter, cream the butter and sugar until light and fluffy. Stir together all the dry ingredients. Break the egg, stir it lightly and add it slowly to the creamed butter and sugar. Incorporate each addition fully before adding more. By hand, lightly fold in a quarter of the dry ingredients followed by a third of the buttermilk. Add these alternately, ending with the last quarter of the dry ingredients until the batter is well mixed, but not over-beaten. Pour the batter over the pears and bake in the oven for 40 minutes, or until the cake is firm to the touch.

Remove from the oven and cool for at least 10 minutes.

Loosen the cake from the sides of the tin and invert it onto a rimmed plate. Most of the juices should have been absorbed by the pears but if any are left in the tin, spoon them onto the cake.

Serve the cake warm, sliced into individual portions and arranged on warm plates with whipped cream and/or toffee or caramel sauce on the side.

strawberry and mascarpone torte

A step further with the old strawberries and cream idea, this torte really shows off some of Ireland's best produce. It may seem to take a lot of steps, but is definitely worth it.

Serves 6

900 g (2 lb) strawberries

75 g (2½ oz) caster sugar

1 tablespoon lemon juice

450 g (1 lb) mascarpone cheese

140 g (5 oz) Vanilla Custard Sauce (see page 231) or store-bought crème anglaise

2 tablespoons Grand Marnier

3 eggs, separated

6 tablespoons sugar

1 gelatine leaf, softened in cold water

225 g (8 oz) Savoyard biscuits or sponge fingers

Place 400 g (14 oz) of the strawberries in food processor with the sugar and the lemon juice. Blend to a smooth purée and pass through a fine sieve.

Cut the remaining strawberries into 5 mm (¼ in) slices and toss with a spoonful or two of the sauce, just enough to coat the slices.

In a small bowl, beat half the mascarpone with a wooden spoon until soft. Stir in the pastry cream and 1 tablespoon of the Grand Marnier. Set aside.

Whisk the egg yolks with 3 tablespoons of the sugar in a mixing bowl and set it over a saucepan of simmering water. Continue to whisk until the mixture is quite fluffy and pale in colour (about 5–10 minutes). It should feel warmer than body temperature. Drain the gelatine and whisk it into the egg-yolk mixture. Continue to whisk over the heat until the gelatine is fully dissolved. Remove from the heat, and beat until light and fluffy.

Beat the remaining mascarpone with a wooden spoon until soft and fold into the egg-yolk mixture. Fold in the remaining tablespoon Grand Marnier. Whisk the egg whites with the remaining sugar until stiff and glossy, then fold them into the egg and mascarpone mixture.

Use either a soufflé dish or six 7.5 cm (3 in) soufflé moulds or pastry rings. Line the base(s) with sponge fingers, and soak them heavily with the strawberry sauce. Cover with a single layer of the sliced strawberries. Spoon in a 1 cm (½ in) layer of pastry-cream/mascarpone mix. Add another layer of the sponge fingers but do not soak this layer, it will absorb enough moisture from both below and above. Cover with another single layer of sliced strawberries. The mould(s) should be about half-full by now. Fill to the top with the egg and mascarpone mixture. Place the torte(s) in the fridge to set for at least 2 hours.

If making in a soufflé mould, serve from the mould after it has been well chilled. If making individually, unmould the tortes as carefully as possible and place on plates. Drizzle the strawberry sauce around the tortes and, if you wish, decorate each with a strawberry and a mint sprig. The tortes can be made a day or two ahead and stored in the fridge.

fruit gâteaux with lemon balm

This makes for a delightfully light dessert, as refreshing on the palate as a sorbet yet so much more in texture and appearance. It could just as easily be made in a terrine and sliced into portions.

Serves 6

1 bottle of dry Muscat wine

300 ml (½ pint) Sugar Syrup (see page 231)

1 bunch of fresh lemon balm, leaves removed

4 large grapefruit

8 navel oranges

8 gelatine leaves, soaked in cold water for 10 minutes

Fresh lemon balm or mint sprigs, to decorate

FOR THE SAUCE

300 ml (½ pint) orange juice, strained

100 g (4 oz) caster sugar

½ tablespoon arrowroot or potato flour, dissolved in 3 tablespoons water

2 tablespoons grenadine

Gently infuse the wine, sugar syrup and half the lemon balm leaves in a large saucepan over a medium heat, for about 20 minutes.

Meanwhile, cut away the skin, including the pith, from the grapefruit and oranges. Neatly cut out the segments so that no membrane is left on. Catch the juices and segments in a bowl as you are doing this. It is very important to lay the segments out on a clean tea towel or kitchen paper now, to let the individual segments dry. If you don't do this, the jelly will have trouble adhering to the segments, and the whole thing may fall apart when you unmould it.

Add the softened gelatine to the infusion and stir until it is well dissolved. Strain through a very fine sieve. Allow to cool to room temperature, but the infusion must still be pourable.

Grease six little cups or moulds with a grease spray. Pour just enough of the infusion into each one to cover the base to a depth of about 3 mm (⅛ in). Carefully lay two or three leaves of lemon balm on this layer. Keep in mind that, when presented, the bottom of the mould will be on top, so place the leaves with the vein sides facing up.

Taking the orange and grapefruit segments, lay them on this base, alternating the two to provide a contrast of colours. Put them in rather tightly, not pressing them down or in, but just making them fit snugly together. Ladle or pour in the infusion, letting it fill all the gaps. Gently tap the moulds once or twice to remove any air bubbles, and fill each mould to the rim. Place in the fridge for at least 2 hours, until the gâteaux seem completely set.

To make the sauce, put the orange juice and sugar in a small saucepan, and bring to the boil over a medium-high heat. Stir in the dissolved arrowroot or potato flour and return to the boil. Simmer for 1 minute just to ensure that the arrowroot or potato flour is well dissolved. Remove from the heat and strain through a fine sieve. Add the grenadine and chill in the fridge. The chilled sauce shouldn't be too thick in consistency, yet not too runny either.

Unmould the gâteaux onto plates by running a very sharp knife around the edge of the moulds and, if necessary, quickly dip the moulds into very hot water. This slightly melts the jelly, releasing the edges and bottom. Surround each gâteaux with the orange sauce and decorate with a sprig of lemon balm or mint.

Baking is yet another great tradition of the Irish kitchen. These recipes are really just a tempting introduction to the wealth of baked specialities that have been around for so many centuries. Some are simple griddle breads, whipped up in seconds flat; others will need a little more time, but should not daunt the average domestic cook. All are mouthwatering reminders of days gone by, when every hearth and kitchen smugly sent out enticing aromas of oven-fresh breads, biscuits and cakes.

Oats, barley and rye were a lot more popular in older times. They still grow well in this climate and lend themselves to both man and beast as wholesome, nutritious fare. Nowadays, wheat is common too, although it is a 'softer' variety, with a lower gluten content, than the type usually used for breads on the Continent. It is perfect for pastries though, giving tender, delicate results.

Historically, each Irish village and town had its own mill, usually water-driven, so grains were fresh milled and full of flavour. Most kitchens had only hearths, not ovens, so the breads that developed were baked on griddles, or in 'Dutch' oven type pots. Yeast is a recent blow-in. Buttermilk and baking soda were the raising agents used in the past. Each of these has its own benefits, but Jeanne would point out that when she uses buttermilk in her cakes or biscuits she feels that not only does it ensure a tender crumb, but it also gives great keeping qualities. Another point to digest is that anyone with yeast allergies can still feast themselves on soda breads.

Our family goes through almost a loaf of wheaten bread a day. Wheaten flour, which is a quite coarsely milled product, might be hard to come by outside Ireland. If you can't find it, try a wholemeal flour with a handful or two of roughly chopped wheat flakes as a replacement (wheat flakes are available in health stores everywhere). We use a cast-iron frying pan as a substitute for a griddle and, believe us, knocking off a batch of soda farls is as easy as making pancakes. We love to add fruits to our muffins and teabreads; the Irish Bramley is a fantastic apple for baking. It is tart in flavour and cooks out to an apple-sauce type of consistency, so just imagine the moistness and flavour it will lend to your baking. Feel free to use whatever berries are in season or available in your neck of the woods.

A great way to break into the idea of baking at home is to get the kids involved. I guarantee they will adore the experience, especially making soda breads, which are virtually foolproof.

baking

passion fruit meringue tarts

We love the exploding flavour and aroma of passion fruit. It pairs well with the buttery flakiness of puff pastry, and the topping of meringue is just the type of sweet stickiness that the Irish love in their puds.

Serves 8

250 g (9 oz) Puff Pastry (see pages 233–4), rolled to about 5 mm (¼ in) thick and cut into 8 rounds about 10 cm (4 in) in diameter, chilled

2 egg yolks, beaten

4 egg whites

85 g (3 oz) sugar

2–3 tablespoons caster sugar, to decorate

6–8 ripe passion fruit, to decorate

FOR THE PASSION FRUIT FILLING

2 eggs

2 egg yolks

6–8 tablespoons passion fruit concentrate

2 teaspoons lemon juice

125 g (4½ oz) unsalted butter

Preheat the oven to 190°C/375°F/Gas 5.

To prepare the puff pastry discs, remove them from the fridge and place on a flat baking tray. Brush the tops of each circle of pastry with the beaten egg, making sure it doesn't drip over the sides as this will prevent the pastry from rising evenly. Using a template about 2.5 cm (1 in) smaller than the diameter of the rounds, mark a light line around this smaller circle with the tip of a sharp knife. This will act as a guide to cutting out the inside after baking. Bake the rounds in the preheated oven until golden brown. To help the pastries rise evenly, place a greased cooling rack over them. Remove it carefully when they are cooked.

With a sharp knife, cut around the imprint of the smaller circle on each round, and scoop out the centre of the pastry, being careful not to cut right through to the bottom. This forms a hollow for the filling. Place the rounds on a wire rack to cool.

To cook the passion fruit filling, simply place all the ingredients in a small saucepan and whisk together over a low heat until thick. This will take about 15 minutes, whisking continually. Remove from the heat, strain through a fine sieve and chill.

When ready to assemble, whisk the egg whites, starting slowly. After 30 seconds, increase the speed and watch. When the whites have become opaque and are starting to firm, drizzle in the caster sugar a little at a time. When it is all in, whisk at high speed for 1 minute. The resulting meringue should be shiny, glossy and firm, but not dry and breaking apart.

Place a generous spoonful or two of the filling in the hollow in each pastry round. Then, with the aid of a spatula, or even using a piping bag, top with lots of the meringue (it should go right to the edges of the pastry and form a little mound over the filling). Sprinkle with the remaining sugar. This helps the meringue to colour evenly. Bake for about 5 minutes. If the meringue cooks too long, it will go tough and rubbery. Remove from the oven when the meringue is nicely brown.

To serve, halve the fresh passion fruit and squeeze a generous amount of the seeds and juice over the hot tarts. Serve at once.

apricot and almond tart

We love the way the rich buttery juices of the caramel and apricot blend together as this tart bakes. When the tart is turned out all that flavour is there, ready to soak into the pastry and moist almond cream. This is definitely another of Paul's favourites...

Serves 8

200 g (8 oz) almond shortcrust pastry

125 g (4½ oz) sugar

2 tablespoons butter

A squeeze of lemon juice

12 fresh, ripe apricots, weighing about 1 kg (2 lb 4 oz) in total, (good-quality canned ones can be substituted)

10 amaretti biscuits, weighing about 60 g (generous 2 oz), roughly ground or chopped

Cream, to serve

FOR THE ALMOND CREAM

125 g (4½ oz) unsalted butter

125 g (4½ oz) sugar

125 g (4½ oz) ground almonds

1 heaped teaspoon plain white flour

2 eggs, lightly beaten

A dash of almond extract or 1 tablespoon of Amaretto liqueur

FOR THE APRICOT ORANGE SAUCE

125 g (4½ oz) dried apricots

100 g (4 oz) sugar

A slice of lemon

Juice of 2 oranges, or to taste

First, make the almond cream, because it should rest for several hours before being used. Whisk the butter and sugar until light and fluffy. Add the ground almonds and flour. Mix well. Slowly add the eggs, ensuring that each addition blends in well. Add the almond extract or Amaretto and place in the fridge.

Roll the shortcrust pastry out to a thickness of 3 mm (⅛ in). Trim into a circle about 5 cm (2 in) larger than the 24 cm (9½ in) cake tin in which you will assemble the pie. Place in the fridge.

Place 75 ml (2½ fl oz) of water in a heavy-based saucepan, add the sugar and cook to a medium caramel over a medium-high heat. Once there is a good golden colour, stop the cooking process by adding a few more spoonfuls of water. Swirl in the butter and lemon juice. Pour the caramel into the base of the tin. Leave to cool.

Preheat the oven to 180°C/350°F/Gas 4.

Skin, halve and stone the apricots. Arrange them on the caramel, rounded-side down. Sprinkle the amaretti biscuits over the fruit.

Place the almond cream in a piping bag and pipe over the apricot halves evenly and to a thickness of about 2 cm (¾ in). Lastly, take the pastry from the fridge and carefully arrange it on top of the almond cream, tucking a good 2 cm (1 in) or so of crust in between the sides of the tin and the almond cream. Bake in the oven for 30 minutes. Reduce the heat to 160°C/325°F/Gas 3 and bake for another 30 minutes.

Remove from the oven and, with the aid of a palette knife, check that all sides of the tart are released from the sides of the tin. Place a large plate over the tin and turn the tin upside down. Leave the tin for 30 seconds or so before removing it, to aid the tart being released from the tin (the steam from the heat helps).

To make the apricot orange sauce, place all the ingredients in a saucepan over a medium-low heat. Simmer until the apricots are very tender. Remove from the heat and purée in a food processor. Sieve the sauce into a bowl and add more orange juice to taste, or to the desired consistency (the natural starches of apricots will give a thick result).

To serve, cut the tart into wedge-shaped portions and serve with some of the sauce and a dollop of cream.

irish coffee tart

A dark and sumptuous tart with smooth chocolate as the background for the coffee and whiskey flavours. The ultimate touch is the Baileys Irish Cream in the topping, but you could leave that out if you wish.

Serves 8–10

125 g (4½ oz) unsalted butter, diced

25 g (1 oz) golden brown sugar

50 g (2 oz) sugar

125 g (4½ oz) plain white flour

1½ tablespoons cornflour

A pinch of salt

175 g (6 oz) hazelnuts, toasted and roughly chopped

Butter, for greasing

Chocolate Sauce (see page 230) and lightly whipped cream, to serve

FOR THE FILLING

300 ml (½ pint) double cream

100 ml (3½ fl oz) single cream

100 ml (3½ fl oz) Bushmills Irish whiskey

2 tablespoons coffee essence or very strong coffee

300 g (10 oz) dark chocolate, finely chopped

100 g (4 oz) milk chocolate, finely chopped

2 eggs, beaten

FOR THE TOPPING

½ gelatine leaf or 1 teaspoon powdered gelatine

250 ml (9 fl oz) whipping cream

140 g (5 oz) icing sugar

4 tablespoons Baileys Irish Cream

Preheat the oven to 160°C/325°F/Gas 3.

Process the butter, both sugars, flour, cornflour, salt and half the hazelnuts to a crumbly texture in a food processor. Pat in an even layer into the base of a greased 23 cm (9 in) springform tin. Bake for 20 minutes, until golden brown. Remove from the oven and leave to cool.

Reduce the oven temperature to 150°C/300°F/Gas 2.

For the filling, bring the double and single creams to the boil in a saucepan, then remove from the heat and add the Bushmills and coffee essence or coffee. Cool slightly before stirring in both the chopped chocolates. Stir and, when the chocolates have melted, stir in the eggs. Pour the filling over the base and bake on the centre shelf of the oven for about 20 minutes, until just set but still slightly wobbly at the centre. Remove from the oven and leave to cool completely.

To make the topping, soften the leaf gelatine (or dissolve the powdered gelatine, if using) in 2 tablespoons of water for a few minutes, then heat gently to dissolve. Set aside to cool slightly. Whip the cream until it forms soft peaks and sift in the icing sugar. Mix in the gelatine and Baileys Irish cream. Spread in an even layer over the chocolate filling and leave to set.

Serve in slices, with some chocolate sauce drizzle over and around, lightly whipped cream on the side and the remaining hazelnuts scattered over.

latticed rhubarb and strawberry tart

A tart like this takes us back to when home-baking was common and the time given to it was not rushed or limited. Yes, it takes a bit of care and love to get this tart built, but what a wonderful dessert to present to anyone, especially if you are out to impress.

Serves 8

500 g (1 lb 2 oz) rhubarb, cut into about 2.5 cm (1 in) pieces

140–250 g (5–9 oz) sugar

Flour, for dusting

450 g (1 lb) Sweet Shortcrust Pastry (see page 235)

Butter, for greasing

450 g (1 lb) strawberries, hulled and halved or quartered

2–3 tablespoons cornflour

2 egg yolks, beaten in 1 tablespoon water

Clotted cream or whipped cream, to serve

Toss the pieces of rhubarb with half the sugar and leave in a colander over a bowl for about 1 hour. Drain most of the excess juices out of the rhubarb (to prevent them making the pastry soggy) until around 1–2 tablespoons are left.

When you are ready to roll out the pastry, flour the work surface lightly, divide the pastry into two halves, and roll out 2 rounds of about 3 mm (⅛ in) thick. Both rounds should be about 28 cm (11 in) in diameter. Using a straight edge, a knife or a pastry wheel cut one of the rounds into strips about 1 cm (½ in) wide. You will need to have about 14 strips.

To lattice the strips, place a sheet of greaseproof paper on the back of a baking tray. Position 6–7 parallel strips of pastry lengthways with about 2.5 cm (1 in) between each of them. Fold alternate strips back halfway and lay another strip of pastry crossways. Lay it over the unfolded strips and position it on the greaseproof paper, next to where the folded strips turn back. Now put the folded strips back in place. Fold back the strips that now lie underneath the crossways piece and lay down a second crossways piece as before, 2.5 cm (1 in) from the first one. Unfold the folded strips and continue the process until the lattice is formed. Keep its diameter to about 28 cm (11 in). Chill the lattice and the remaining round in the fridge for at least 20 minutes.

Preheat the oven to 180°C/350°F/Gas 4 and grease a medium-sized slope-sided pie tin.

Mix the drained rhubarb with the strawberries and the remaining sugar. Take about half of the reserved juices and place them in a small saucepan over a medium heat. Dissolve the cornflour in a little water and add to the juices. Boil for 2 minutes, until thickened. Add to the rhubarb and mix well.

Take both pieces of pastry out of the fridge. Line the pie tin with the full round.

Brush the lattice with the egg-yolk wash. Pour the filling into the pie base and brush the rim of the base with water. Remove the lattice and paper from the baking tray and align over the pie tin. Slide the paper from under the lattice and carefully slide the lattice over the filling. Pinch the edges of the lattice and the base together and trim off all excess pastry. The edge can be pinched decoratively with your thumb and forefinger.

Bake in the oven for about 40 minutes, until the pastry is golden brown and the fruit is tender. When you think the pie is done, try to take a peek at the pie base or check the sides of the pie crust to be sure it is cooked. You may have to reduce the oven heat slightly and leave the tart in for another 15 minutes or so. Remove the tart from the oven and set aside for 20–30 minutes.

Cut into slices and serve with clotted cream, if available – whipped cream will also taste great.

blueberry pancakes

Don't wait until you have blueberries to try out these little beauties – raspberries work just as well, as do strawberries.

Makes 12–14 pancakes

250 g (9 oz) self-raising flour

1½ teaspoons bicarbonate of soda

1¼ teaspoons salt

2–4 tablespoons sugar

2 eggs

500 ml (18 fl oz) buttermilk, at room temperature

2 tablespoons melted butter

2 tablespoons golden syrup

About 200 g (8 oz) fresh or frozen blueberries

Oil or butter, for frying

Maple syrup or lemon juice and sugar, to serve

Sift or stir together the flour, baking powder, salt and sugar in a medium-sized bowl. Add the eggs and liquids and stir gently with a whisk until the mixture is fairly homogenous. Do not over-beat, as this will make the pancakes very tough. Let the batter rest for about 20–30 minutes. Add the blueberries just before you start to cook the pancakes.

To cook, heat a non-stick frying pan over a medium heat. Grease lightly with the oil or butter. Pour several ladlefuls of the batter into the pan, leaving enough space for them to spread a little. After 3–4 minutes, the edges will be golden brown and the tops will be covered in little air bubbles. Turn the pancakes over and cook them for another 2 minutes. You can keep the cooked pancakes warm on a plate in a low oven, while you cook the remaining pancakes.

Serve with maple syrup, or lemon juice and sugar.

apple, cinnamon and hazelnut cake

A moist and comforting cake that is not too sweet, this freezes well and can be served with a Toffee Sauce (see page 230), or simply with whipped cream. If you prefer, the sultanas can be omitted, but we love the texture and moistness they add.

Serves 10

85 g (3 oz) sultanas
5 tablespoons cognac
Grated zest and juice of 1 lemon
700 g (1 lb 9 oz) Granny Smiths
200 g (8 oz) unsalted butter, plus extra for greasing
300 g (10 oz) sugar
2 eggs
2 teaspoons vanilla essence
375 g (13 oz) plain white flour
1 teaspoon bicarbonate of soda
1 teaspoon baking powder
2 teaspoons ground cinnamon
A pinch of salt
100 g (4 oz) hazelnuts, roughly chopped
Icing sugar, sifted, for dusting
Toffee Sauce (see page 230) or whipped cream, to serve

Soak the sultanas in the cognac for several hours or overnight.

Preheat the oven to 180°C/350°F/Gas 4.

Place the lemon juice in a bowl, peel the apples and turn them in the lemon juice to prevent them from discolouring.

Liberally grease a 23 cm (9 in) springform tin. Quarter and core 1–2 apples and cut each quarter into 5–6 slices. Arrange the slices in concentric circles in the tin. Grate the remaining apples and toss in the lemon juice. Leave to drain in a colander.

Cream the butter and sugar together until light and fluffy. Break the eggs into a small bowl and stir in the vanilla essence. Beat this into the butter and sugar a little at a time, making sure each addition is incorporated before adding more.

Sift the flour, soda, baking powder, cinnamon and salt together. Add the lemon zest. Fold into the creamed mixture, along with the grated apples, soaked sultanas and hazelnuts. Carefully spread the batter over the sliced apples in the tin.

Bake for an hour, covering the edges of the cake with foil if they brown too quickly. Lower the oven temperature to 160°C/325°F/Gas 3 for the last 15 minutes of cooking. The cake is done when a skewer pushed into the centre comes out clean. Cool for 15 minutes in the tin before carefully turning out on to a rack.

Preheat the grill to hot.

To serve, dust the top of the cake liberally with the icing sugar and slide the cake under the grill for 1–2 minutes to glaze the apple slices. Serve with some toffee sauce or whipped cream.

Opposite: Spiced Ginger Cake with Cream Cheese Frosting (rear, see page 215), Lemon Pound Cake with Gingered Rhubarb Compote (middle, see page 214), Apple, Cinnamon and Hazelnut Cake (front)

lemon pound cake with gingered rhubarb compote

The buttermilk in this loaf improves its keeping quality so much. In fact, we prefer the cake on the second day, when the flavours have had time to deepen and settle. Fresh spring rhubarb doesn't need much tampering with, but ginger seems a natural partner.

Serves 8

240 g (scant 9 oz) unsalted butter, plus extra for greasing

400 g (14 oz) sugar

Grated zest and juice of 1 lemon

4 eggs

360 g (generous 12 oz) plain white flour

2 teaspoons baking powder

A pinch of salt

250 ml (9 fl oz) buttermilk

FOR THE SYRUP GLAZE

6 tablespoons fresh lemon juice

175 g (6 oz) icing sugar

FOR THE GINGERED RHUBARB COMPOTE

225 g (8 oz) fresh young rhubarb, cleaned

60–100 g (2–4 oz) caster sugar

½ teaspoon root ginger, peeled and grated

Grated zest of 1 orange

Preheat the oven to 180°C/350°F/Gas 4. Grease a 450 g/1 lb cake or loaf tin.

Cream the butter, sugar and lemon zest in a bowl together until light and fluffy. Stop once or twice and scrape down the sides of the bowl with a spatula, to ensure that the mixture is homogenous.

Break the eggs into a small bowl and stir them gently together. Slowly add the eggs to the butter/sugar mixture, a spoonful at a time, making sure each addition is incorporated before adding more. Adding just a tablespoon of the flour at this stage helps the eggs to bind with the butter/sugar without curdling.

Sift the flour, baking powder and salt together and fold in by hand, one third at a time, alternating with the buttermilk. Lastly, fold in the lemon juice. Pour the mixture into the baking tin and place in the centre of the oven. Bake for at least 1¼ hours. If you are using a loaf tin it may take 1½ hours. The cake is done when a toothpick inserted into the centre comes out clean. Remove from the oven and allow to cool for 10 minutes.

For the syrup glaze, briefly boil the lemon juice and icing sugar until the sugar has dissolved. Do not continue to boil or the syrup will thicken too much.

When the cake has cooled slightly, remove it from the tin and, using a skewer, poke holes all over the top. Gently ladle the glaze over the top, a little at a time so that the all of the glaze is absorbed rather than just running off the sides.

To make the gingered rhubarb compote, slice the rhubarb stalks into pieces about 3 cm (1¼ in) in length. Place in a small saucepan over a medium-high heat with the sugar, ginger and orange zest. (The exact amount of sugar will depend on the rhubarb. Use more or less ginger depending on your own taste. Some people prefer just a hint, some like a strong flavour.) Almost immediately, the rhubarb will release some liquid and this will prevent the fruit from sticking on the bottom of the pan — but watch carefully for the first minute and stir a bit if necessary to stop it catching. Cook until the rhubarb is tender. Depending on its thickness and age this will take 5–10 minutes. It's best to take it off the heat while the pieces still hold as it will continue to cook as it cools. If overcooked, the rhubarb will turn to mush. This will still taste great but we prefer the compote with a bit of texture.

spiced ginger cake with cream cheese frosting

This moist and tender cake would be perfect with a cup of mid-morning tea, with or without the frosting. It could equally hold its own on a sweet trolley. Think about serving it with a plum compote or fresh orange segments, if you are really out to impress.

Serves 8–12

175 g (6 oz) unsalted butter, plus extra for greasing

100 g (4 oz) golden brown sugar

2 tablespoons grated root ginger

4 egg yolks

250 g (9 oz) plain white flour

1 tablespoon ground ginger

$^{1}/_{2}$ teaspoon ground cinnamon

$^{1}/_{4}$ teaspoon grated nutmeg

$^{1}/_{4}$ teaspoon ground cloves

$1^{1}/_{2}$ teaspoons bicarbonate of soda

200 ml (7 fl oz) molasses or black treacle

100 ml ($3^{1}/_{2}$ fl oz) soured cream

8 egg whites

45 g ($1^{1}/_{2}$ oz) caster sugar

FOR THE CREAM CHEESE FROSTING

225 g (8 oz) packet of cream cheese, at room temperature

75 g ($2^{1}/_{2}$ oz) unsalted butter, at room temperature

1 teaspoon vanilla essence

400 g (14 oz) icing sugar, sifted

Preheat the oven to 180°C/350°F/Gas 4 and butter a 23 cm (9 in) diameter springform cake tin.

Cream the butter, sugar and ginger until light and fluffy. Slowly add the egg yolks, making sure each addition is incorporated before adding more. Sift together all the dry ingredients. Stir together the molasses or treacle and soured cream. By hand fold the dry ingredients and the cream mixture alternately.

Whisk the egg whites with the caster sugar until they are shiny, glossy and firm, and fold into the cake mixture. Take care to ensure they are well mixed in or there will be streaks in the cake.

Pour the mixture into the cake tin and bake for about 45–55 minutes, until the cake is pulling away from the sides of the tin and a toothpick inserted in the centre comes out clean. Remove from the oven and cool for 10 minutes before turning out onto a wire rack.

To make the cream cheese frosting, cream the cheese and butter together in a food processor until smooth. Add the vanilla and sugar and beat until smooth. This frosting is very rich and thick.

When the cake is completely cool, coat with the cream cheese frosting.

decadent chocolate brownies

There's really absolutely nothing Irish about these rich fudgy brownies, but I've yet to meet an Irishman who doesn't fall for them. Besides, every cookery book should contain at least one killer chocolate recipe.

Serves 8

100 g (4 oz) plain white flour
140 g (5 oz) icing sugar
1 heaped teaspoon cocoa
140 g (5 oz) dark chocolate
100 g (4 oz) unsalted butter, melted
2 tablespoons golden syrup
2 eggs
1½ teaspoons vanilla essence
45 g (1½ oz) chopped hazelnuts, roasted, skinned and chopped
Whipped cream or vanilla ice-cream, to serve

Preheat the oven to 180°C/350°F/Gas 4. Grease a 25 cm (10 in) square baking tin.

Sift the dry flour, icing sugar and cocoa into a large bowl. Melt the chocolate carefully in a bowl over a saucepan of simmering water. Add the butter and golden syrup and mix well. Remove from the heat.

When the chocolate mixture has cooled to lukewarm, stir in the eggs and vanilla. Fold in the sifted dry ingredients and stir rather quickly until smooth. Fold in the hazelnuts.

Pour the mixture into the baking tin and bake for 30–45 minutes. The top and edges will be crusty. The inside will be slightly gooey, but not runny. Remove from the oven and leave to cool slightly in the tin

Cut into eight squares, and serve while still warm with a dollop of whipped cream or, even better, vanilla ice-cream. The brownies keeps for a couple days if wrapped in clingfilm.

oatmeal muffins

For those who can't face up to a steaming bowl of porridge every morning, these muffins offer a quick, easy and just as healthy alternative. They could be sweeter if desired, but they have a wholesome nutritious feeling when made as follows.

Makes 24 muffins

225 g (8 oz) rolled oats
(old-fashioned style)
700 ml (1¼ pints) buttermilk
300 g (10 oz) plain white flour
1½ teaspoons baking soda
1½ teaspoons salt
200 g (8 oz) soft brown sugar
Grated zest and juice of 1 lemon
3 tablespoons melted butter
3 eggs, beaten
100 g (4 oz) chopped dates, tossed in
just enough flour to coat
140 g (5 oz) finely chopped apples,
tossed in the lemon juice

Leave the oats to soak in the buttermilk overnight (or at least a couple of hours). **Preheat the oven** to 180°C/350°F/Gas 4. Line two 12-hole muffin trays with paper muffin cases.

Sift the flour, soda and salt together into a big bowl. Combine with the sugar and the lemon zest. Mix in the oat mixture by hand. Stir in the butter and eggs, until only just combined. Lastly, fold in the dates and apples. Note that the apples must be chopped quite finely to ensure that they cook completely in the muffins' short cooking time.

Fill the prepared muffin cases generously, to about two-thirds full. Bake for about 17–20 minutes. Muffin tins can vary in size, so keep that in mind.

Cool the muffins on wire racks, then eat immediately, or keep in an airtight container.

gypsy creams

This is another one of those treasured recipes that has been handed on to Jeanne from Paul's mum and aunt, who had it from their mum. It is the perfect accompaniment to afternoon tea.

Makes about 24 biscuits = 12 gypsy creams

125 g (4½ oz) unsalted butter
125 g (4½ oz) vegetable shortening
100 g (4 oz) caster sugar
2 teaspoons golden syrup
2 teaspoons bicarbonate of soda
250 g (9 oz) self-raising flour
2 cups rolled oat flakes
Flour, for dusting
24 walnuts, lightly toasted and skinned, to decorate

FOR THE ICING

125 g (4½ oz) unsalted butter
250 g (9 oz) icing sugar, sifted
A drop or two of coffee essence or instant coffee dissolved in a few drops of water

Preheat the oven to 160ºC/325ºF/Gas 3.

Cream together the butter, margarine and sugar until light and fluffy. Meanwhile, mix 5 teaspoons of boiling water with the golden syrup. Pour this into the mixture and beat together. Sift the soda together with the self-raising flour. Fold into the butter mixture by hand. Fold in the oats and make sure everything is well incorporated.

On a lightly floured surface, roll the dough out to a thickness of about 1 cm (½ in) and, using a cutter about 4 cm (1½ in) in diameter, cut out 24 rounds. Place them on an ungreased baking tray and bake for approximately 12 minutes, until golden brown. Cool on wire racks.

To make the icing, simply cream together the butter and icing sugar in a food processor until light and fluffy. Add the coffee essence or instant coffee. The icing should not be either too runny or too thick. It should have a nice spreadable consistency, similar to the texture of peanut butter. When the biscuits are cool, sandwich two together with the icing and continue until you have 12 gypsy creams.

We like to decorate each gypsy cream with a little blob of the icing and top this with a walnut.

malted granary bread with dried cranberries and walnuts

This bread makes the tastiest toast about. Feel free to use hazelnuts instead of walnuts, but do toast them first to bring out their flavour.

Makes two 450 g (1 lb) loaves

Vegetable oil, for greasing

650 g (1 lb 7 oz) malted granary flour, plus extra for dusting

½ teaspoon salt

7 g (¼ oz) sachet of easy-blend dried yeast

2 tablespoons malt extract (optional)

1 tablespoon unsalted butter, melted

50 g (2 oz) dried cranberries

50 g (2 oz) walnuts, toasted, skinned and roughly chopped

3 tablespoons sugar

Preheat the oven to 200°C/400°F/Gas 6.

Grease two 450 g (1 lb) loaf tins.

Place the flour, salt and yeast in the bowl of a food processor. Add 370 ml (13 fl oz) water, malt extract and melted butter to the flour and yeast mixture, and mix either with a dough-hook attachment on medium speed for about 5 minutes, or by hand, turning it out onto a lightly floured surface and kneading it for at least 10 minutes. The dough should be smooth, elastic and pliable. Add the cranberries and nuts and mix again until they are thoroughly interspersed. Turn the dough into a greased bowl, cover with clingfilm and leave to rise in a warm place until doubled in size, about 1 hour.

Turn out onto a lightly floured work surface and knead for several minutes to knock back. Split the dough into two equal pieces. Flatten out the pieces and form into oblong ovals to fit the loaf tins by rolling them up towards yourself.

Place with the seam towards the bottom of the tin. Cover with clingfilm and leave to rise again until double, about 30 minutes.

Heat 3 tablespoons of water and the sugar in the microwave or in a small saucepan, bringing to the boil and simmering for 1 minute, to make a little sugar syrup.

Just before placing the risen loaves in the oven, remove the clingfilm and brush the tops with the syrup. After the first 10 minutes of baking, brush the loaves again (without removing them from the oven if possible). Bake for about 45–55 minutes, until the bottom of each loaf sounds hollow when tapped.

Remove from the oven and cool on wire racks.

The bread will keep very well for several days if wrapped in clingfilm.

guinness and onion bread

This tasty, savoury bread goes well with winter soups or makes a great base for tasty sandwiches. Substitute vegetable oil or melted butter for the walnut oil and omit the walnuts, if you prefer.

Makes two 450 g (1 lb) loaves

7 g (¼ oz) sachet of easy-blend dried yeast
1 teaspoon sugar
550 g (1 lb 4 oz) strong white bread flour, plus extra for dusting
200 g (8 oz) strong wholemeal flour
1 teaspoon salt
440 ml (16 fl oz) can of Guinness, at room temperature
2 tablespoons walnut oil, plus extra for greasing
½ medium onion, finely diced
½ tablespoon unsalted butter

FOR THE TOPPING
1 large egg, lightly beaten with 1 tablespoon milk (optional)
2 tablespoons roughly chopped walnuts
Cornmeal (polenta), if available, for dusting

Place the yeast, sugar and 4 tablespoons of warm, not hot, water in a small bowl and leave for 10 minutes, until frothy, foamy and thick. If the yeast has not started to develop after this amount of time, it will not, so throw it away and start again. If the water is too hot it could kill the yeast, so be sure to just have it warm, about body temperature (also the yeast could be too old, so check the use-by date).

Place the two flours and salt in the bowl of a food processor. When the yeast has proved, add it, the Guinness and the walnut oil and, with the dough-hook attachment, mix for about 5 minutes on low. The dough should not be too wet or sticky. If it is, add more white flour, a little at a time until it is pliable, rather smooth and elastic.

Coat a large bowl with a bit of walnut oil and put the dough in. Cover the bowl with clingfilm and leave to rise until double in size, about 1 hour.

While the dough is rising, gently sauté the onion in the butter until it is soft and transparent. Drain and leave to cool.

Turn the risen dough out onto a lightly floured work surface and punch it down. Fold in the onions and work the dough for about 2 minutes, turning it over on itself in thirds. Try to not tear the dough but just to stretch it; this is to work the gluten. Divide the dough into two and roll into two freeform oblong loaves. This is done by flattening the dough and then rolling it towards you, pulling it tightly but, again, not so tightly as to tear the dough. The outer surface will be pulled taut and this will help the loaf to hold its shape during baking.

Place the loaves on a baking sheet and cover loosely with greased clingfilm. Do not grease the sheet. It is best to dust the sheet first with a fine layer of cornmeal, if possible (flour burns too easily). Leave to rise until doubled in size, about 40 minutes.

Preheat the oven to 200°C/400°F/Gas 6. Place an old roasting tray on the bottom of the oven. Let it get nice and hot.

Remove the clingfilm. Lightly brush the loaves with the egg wash, or even just water, and sprinkle the walnuts over the tops of the loaves. Using a very sharp knife, slice down the centre of each loaf, to a depth of about 1 cm (½ in). Place the loaves in the oven and, at the same time, pour about 500 ml (18 fl oz) of water into the roasting tin. The water will start to evaporate immediately, causing the whole oven to steam up. This will give an immediate boost to the loaves' rising. If the tops of the loaves are browning too much after about 30 minutes, turn the oven down to 190ºC/375ºF/Gas 5. The loaves should be done after about 50 minutes. Tap the bottom of each and, if it sounds hollow, it is done.

Remove the loaves from the oven and cool on wire racks.

crusty farmhouse white bread

There's nothing like the heady aroma of bread fresh from the oven. It is a balanced harmony of simple ingredients and truly worth every shred of effort involved in making it. Bake the loaves in tins or in any shape you like.

Makes two 450 g (1 lb) loaves

25 g (1 oz) fresh yeast or two 7 g (¼ oz) packets of easy-blend dried yeast
1 kg (2 lb 4 oz) strong white flour
25 g (1 oz) salt
50 g (2 oz) unsalted butter
Vegetable oil, for greasing

Blend the yeast into 300 ml (½ pint) of the warm water and leave for 10 minutes until it becomes frothy and foamy. Put the flour, salt and butter into a food processor and, with the dough hook, process on medium speed, and add the yeast liquid and the remaining 600 ml (1 pint) of water together. Beat on medium speed until the dough has come together, looks rather shiny and has a nice elasticity. It should not be sticky.

Turn out into a big clean bowl and cover the bowl with clingfilm. Leave to rise at room temperature for 1½–2 hours until the dough has doubled in size.

If you prefer a more developed flavour, and have the time, punch down the dough again, form into a ball and return to the bowl to rise a second time. This time need not be quite as long, 1–1½ hours should do.

Grease two 450 g (1 lb) loaf tins or two baking sheets. To form loaves to be baked in tins, you don't really have to punch down the dough. The shaping of the loaf will usually dispel the bubbles sufficiently and reactivate the gluten and yeast. First, divide the dough in two. Flatten the first piece, using the heel of your hand. Fold the dough over on itself. Basically, you are rolling a long cylinder shape. Roll it back and forth a bit to smooth the surface. When you place it in the greased tin, the seam should be on the bottom. Repeat with the other piece of dough. Cover the tins with clingfilm and leave to rise until doubled in size.

If you are forming loaves to be baked on a flat baking sheet, i.e. round or oval loaves, you may want to punch down the dough a little more. Simply lift and slap the dough down a few times on your work surface, folding it over on itself in between. Divide the dough in two. With your two hands working one of the pieces in a counterclockwise rotary action, roll the piece until the seam is tucked underneath, and the whole surface is smooth and taut. Place on a greased sheet. Repeat with the other half. Cover the loaves loosely with greased clingfilm and leave to rise until doubled in size.

Preheat the oven to 200°C/400°F/Gas 6.

Just before putting the loaves into the hot oven remove the clingfilm and slash the surfaces with a very sharp knife or razor. Be firm when cutting the slashes – besides being decorative, they make for more crust, which some people prefer.

Bake for 15 minutes and then reduce the temperature to 180°C/350°F/Gas 4 for 30 minutes, to ensure the crust does not brown too much. Spraying the loaves generously with a mister before putting them into the oven will improve the crust by making it crisper.

The loaves are done when the bottom of each one sounds hollow when tapped. Cool on wire racks.

wheaten bread

A wheaten bread is simplicity itself – really; it's becoming familiar with the correct prebaking consistency that is the secret, we think. When you have made it once, it will be easier the next time, then more so the next and so on.

Makes two 900 g (2 lb) loaves

550 g (1 lb 4 oz) coarse wheaten flour
350 g (12 oz) plain white flour
100 g (4 oz) wholemeal flour
1½ teaspoons salt
2½ teaspoons sugar
2 teaspoons bicarbonate of soda
½ teaspoon cream of tartar
½ egg
25 g (1 oz) butter, melted
1 litre (1¾ pints) buttermilk
Vegetable oil, for greasing

Preheat the oven to 200°C/400°F/Gas 6.

Sift the dry ingredients together into a large bowl. After sifting return the coarse grains to the bowl, then add the egg, butter and half the buttermilk. Stir together, but do not beat hard. Add the rest of the buttermilk in small amounts until the mixture is a soft, but not sticky, consistency. Divide between well-greased 900 g (2 lb) loaf tins and place in the centre of the oven. Bake for about 60–90 minutes. If the tops of the loaves are browning too much you may want to turn the oven heat down to 180°C/350°F/Gas 4 for the second half of baking.

Remove the loaves from the oven and turn out onto wire racks. Some people prefer to wrap the loaves in tea towels at this stage to keep a softer crust.

The bread keeps well for a few days if wrapped in clingfilm.

Opposite: Irish Soda Farls (rear, see page 228), Buttermilk Scones (middle left, see page 229), Potato Bread (middle right, see page 228), Wheaten Bread (front)

potato bread

This simple griddle bread is so moist and flavoursome it doesn't really need the rest of
the Ulster Fry-up (see page 137), in our opinion. This is Paul's mother's version.

Serves 4

750 g (1 lb 10 oz) potatoes (e.g. Desiree or
King Edwards), peeled, freshly cooked
and still hot

75 g (2½ oz) plain white flour, plus
extra for dusting

A pinch of salt

30–60 g (generous 1–2 oz) unsalted
butter, melted

Preheat a griddle or heavy-based frying pan until hot.

Mash the potatoes until they are very smooth. While they are still hot, sprinkle
on the flour and salt and mix together. Add the melted butter and knead briefly –
not too much, or the dough will toughen.

On a floured work surface, roll out into a big circle about 1 cm (½ in) thick.
Cut into quarters and cook on the hot griddle or pan for about 3 minutes, until
brown. Turn over and cook the other sides for about 2 minutes.

Potato bread is best eaten fresh, but will keep quite well and can be reheated
the next day.

irish soda farls

These griddle breads are similar to oven-baked soda bread but somehow seem to keep
better. Split in two and served with plenty of jam and butter, they are the perfect match
for a cup of tea.

Serves 4

450 g (1 lb) plain white flour

¾ teaspoon bicarbonate of soda

A pinch of salt

A pinch of sugar

1 teaspoon vegetable oil

450–550 ml (16–19 fl oz) buttermilk

Preheat a griddle or heavy-based frying pan until hot but not smoking. Sift the
dry ingredients together in a bowl and make a well in the centre. Pour in the oil
and 450 ml (16 fl oz) of the buttermilk and mix gently and quickly together. The
resulting dough should be soft and fairly slack; add more buttermilk if necessary.

Turn out onto a work surface and knead lightly for about 1 minute. Work into a
large flat round about 1–1.5 cm (½ – ⅝ in) thick (it may not cook through
properly if it is any thicker). Cut a deep cross through the surface to make four
triangular farls.

The griddle or frying pan should be hot enough to brown a little flour when it is
sprinkled on. The heat should be somewhere between moderate and hot. Place
the farls on the griddle or pan and cook for about 10 minutes on each side.
Obviously, if the crust begins to burn the pan is too hot.

To serve, split each farl in half and spread thickly with butter. When a day or
two old, the farls will be equally delicious toasted.

buttermilk scones

I don't know anyone who can refuse a fresh, well-made scone still just warm from the oven. Add a knob of butter and a spoonful of jam or a dollop of clotted cream. All you need is a cuppa.

Makes about 12 scones

450 g (1 lb) plain white flour, plus extra for greasing
½ tablespoon baking powder
85 g (3 oz) sugar
100 g (4 oz) butter, chilled and diced
1½ eggs
250–300 ml (9–10 fl oz) buttermilk
Vegetable oil, for greasing

Preheat the oven to 200°C/400°F/Gas 6.

Sift the flour with the baking powder and sugar to mix well. Rub in the butter until the mixture resembles fine breadcrumbs (this can be done by hand or in a food processor).

Add the eggs and buttermilk and stir until it comes together. Do not over-beat. The dough should be soft and pliable, but not sticky.

Turn out onto a floured work surface and pat to a thickness of about 4 cm (1½ in). Cut into rounds and place on a greased baking sheet. Brush with milk and bake in a hot oven for 15–20 minutes, until golden on top.

Scones are best eaten on the day they are made.

walnut shortbread

We love the richness the walnuts add to this scrumptious shortbread. Substitute pecans, hazelnuts or even almonds, but be sure to start with fresh nuts and toast them carefully.

Makes 24 wedges or 36 squares

600 g (1 lb 5 oz) plain white flour
200 g (8 oz) sugar
140 g (5 oz) walnuts, toasted, skinned and ground
450 g (1 lb) unsalted butter, chilled and diced

Place all the ingredients in the chilled bowl of a food processor and process until it all comes together. Over-processing will allow the butter to start to melt. Tip out onto a clean surface and quickly, using the heel of your hand, make sure all the ingredients are well mixed. Pat the dough into a round, wrap tightly in clingfilm and place in the fridge for at least 1 hour.

Roll the chilled dough out to a thickness of no more than 1 cm (½ in). Either work it into a round shape and then cut this round into pie-type wedges, or, if preferred, work into a rectangle and cut into square pieces. Either way, transfer the dough onto a baking sheet and chill again for at least 30 minutes.

Preheat the oven to 150°C/300°F/Gas 2.

Bake the shortbread for 25–30 minutes. Ideally, it should take on little, or no colour. Allow to cool and set slightly before removing to a wire rack to finish cooling. Store in an airtight container.

chocolate sauce

Here is a simple chocolate sauce that's easy to whip up and keeps very well in an airtight container in the fridge for a week to ten days. You can flavour it with a liqueur if you wish.

Makes about 250 ml (8 fl oz)

150 ml (5 fl oz) milk
50 ml (2 fl oz) whipping cream
250 g (9 oz) dark chocolate, finely chopped or grated

Bring the milk and cream to the boil. Remove from the heat and leave to cool slightly. Add the chocolate and then stir until well mixed and all the chocolate has melted.

To reheat the sauce melt in a bowl over a pan of simmering water, or at about half power in the microwave for 1–2 minutes.

toffee sauce

A multi-purpose toffee sauce with a real butterscotch flavour, this goes with so many things it is excellent for any chef's repertoire. The sauce can be used warm or cold. It keeps well in the fridge for up to two weeks.

Makes about 250 ml (8 fl oz)

140 g (5 oz) light soft brown sugar
120 ml (4 fl oz) double cream
125 g (4½ oz) unsalted butter
1 teaspoon vanilla essence

Bring all the ingredients to the boil together in a saucepan over a medium-high heat and cook for 2 minutes, stirring continuously. The colour will change to a rich golden hue. Remove from the heat and leave to cool.

vanilla custard sauce

Simple vanilla custard sauce, or crème anglaise, is an essential recipe for anyone interested in pastry and dessert-making. You can build various flavours and spices into this base recipe. Most, like coconut or cinnamon, are infused in the milk before the custard is made. But remember, alcohol and honey should be added only after the custard has been cooked and cooled slightly. This custard can keep in the fridge for up to 5 days depending on how fresh the milk was to start with.

Makes about 600 ml (1 pint)

500 ml (17 fl oz) whole milk
½ vanilla pod, split, or ½ teaspoon vanilla essence
6 egg yolks
125 g (4½ oz) caster sugar

Place the milk in a saucepan with the vanilla pod or vanilla essence and bring to the boil. Set aside to infuse.

Whisk the egg yolks and sugar together in a bowl until lightened in colour and the sugar has dissolved. Whisking continuously, slowly pour the milk into the egg yolk and sugar mixture and whisk together. Pour this mixture back into the pan and cook over a low heat, stirring continuously with a wooden spoon until the mixture has thickened enough to coat the back of the spoon and will hold the line if you run your finger along the middle of the back of the spoon.

When it is to the desired thickness, strain through a fine mesh sieve and cool. You can leave the vanilla pod in the anglaise to continue to increase the flavour or remove it now, scraping all the seeds from inside the pod into the custard.

sugar syrup

This base syrup can be used for sorbets, poaching fruits, soaking sponges, and so on. It keeps indefinitely so it is one of those things to keep on hand as a basic in the kitchen.

Makes 500 ml (17 fl oz)

500 ml (17 fl oz) water
500 g (1 lb 2 oz) sugar
½ vanilla pod or 1 teaspoon vanilla essence
25 g (1 oz) glucose syrup (optional)

Place all the ingredients together in a large pan. Bring to the boil and boil for 2–3 minutes. Skim off any scum that comes to the surface. This is just impurities being released from the sugar. Remove from the heat and leave to cool.

Store in a sealed container in the fridge.

mayonnaise

This is a classic recipe that you can vary by the addition of you favourite herbs, such as basil or parsley.

Serves 4

1 tablespoon Dijon mustard
Salt and freshly ground white pepper
1 tablespoon white wine vinegar
3 egg yolks
500 ml (18 fl oz) vegetable oil or light olive oil

Whisk the mustard, salt, pepper and vinegar in a bowl until the salt has dissolved.

Add the egg yolks and whisk in the oil, very slowly at first, literally drop by drop. As the mayonnaise starts to build up, you can add the oil slightly faster, but always be sure to incorporate each addition fully before adding more. Continue until you have blended in all the oil and the mayonnaise is thick and creamy.

brown chicken stock

Brown chicken stock is one of those invaluable items, to both the professional and the domestic chef. For convenience, make it in large batches. It can be boiled down to concentrate the flavours, and then frozen so it is always on hand.

Makes about 3 litres (5¼ pints)

3 kg (7 lb) chicken bones, wings and legs
500 g (1 lb 2 oz) chopped onions
500 g (1 lb 2 oz) chopped carrots
200 g (8 oz) chopped celery
1 bulb of garlic
100 g (4 oz) tomato purée
1 bouquet garni

Preheat the oven to 200°C/400°F/Gas 6.

Chop the chicken bones with a heavy knife. Roast them in a roasting tin in the preheated oven for about 30 minutes or until nicely brown. Add the vegetables and roast for another 10 minutes.

Transfer the bones and vegetables to a large pan and cover with cold water. Bring to the boil and skim off any fat and scum. Add the tomato purée and bouquet garni. Cover and simmer for 2 hours, skimming frequently. Strain through a fine sieve, then store in an airtight container in the fridge for 1–2 days or in plastic bags in the freezer for 2–3 months.

If you want a stronger, thicker stock, you can reduce the stock by boiling, or just thicken it with a little of your favourite gravy thickener.

puff pastry

We were taught this puff pastry recipe when we worked for Albert Roux. Although we have since tried many other recipes, this is the one we keep coming back to. Puff pastry must be one of the most rewarding pastries to make. You begin with the most basic of ingredients, yet with time and a gentle touch, you end up with the most delightful results. You can make the pastry by hand or in a food processor.

Makes just over 1 kg (2 lb 4 oz)

670 g (1 lb 8 oz) strong plain flour
85 g (3 oz) unsalted butter
1 tablespoon salt
1 egg yolk
1 tablespoon white wine vinegar
600 g (1 lb 5 oz) unsalted butter, diced

Place 500 g (1 lb 2 oz) of the flour together with the smaller batch of butter and the salt in a bowl and rub in the butter. Stir together the egg yolk, 225 ml (8 fl oz) of water and the vinegar, and add them to the bowl. Mix the ingredients together for a good 5–10 minutes until it has all come together into a smooth, shiny dough. Wrap in clingfilm and place in the fridge to rest for 1 hour.

Now place the larger batch of butter with the remaining 175 g (6 oz) of flour into the bowl and mix to a smooth paste-like consistency. Do not mix too much or the butter will get too soft and start to melt. Remove from the bowl and tip out onto a work surface. Pat into a neat rectangle and wrap in clingfilm. Place in the fridge for 1 hour.

After 1 hour, remove both batches. Place the flour-based dough on a floured work surface. Roll it out to a 30 cm (12 in) square. Place the butter-based paste in the centre of the dough and gently, without stretching, fold all 4 sides over as if wrapping the butter-based dough like a present. The object is to enclose the butter completely so that when you start to roll them out, none of the butter can escape or leak out.

Roll the 'package' out carefully but surely until you have a rectangle shape, about 20 x 46 cm (8 x 18 in). Brush off any excess flour and fold the bottom third over, then fold down the top third, the way you would wrap a business letter. Turn this rectangle to be lengthways on the work surface and again, roll out to the dimensions above. Fold into thirds again in the same way, wrap in clingfilm and place in the fridge to chill and rest for 1 hour. This chilling and resting stage is of vital importance. The ingredients must stay cool or their properties will change, consequently your puff pastry would not end up with the right results.

After 1 hour remove from the fridge and roll out twice more in exactly the same way as before. All this rolling is how the many layers that are in puff pastry are formed. If the puff dough is allowed to get too soft, and is forced too much, these layers would be damaged. Wrap in clingfilm and return to the fridge to rest again for 1 hour.

continued overleaf/

/continued from previous page

The last rolling is only one turn, not two like the previous two times. This is the classic number of rolls and turns given to puff pastry. After it has again rested and chilled, it is ready to use. This puff pastry freezes excellently so if you are going to all the effort of making it, be sure to make at least this quantity and then you will have some in the freezer on hand when you need it.

To roll the pastry, take one quarter of the quantity given above to roll at a time. Place on a floured work surface and with a rolling pin, carefully work it out to a thickness of 5 mm (¼ in). This thickness, when cooked, will rise to a good 5 cm (2 in). Place the sheet of puff pastry onto a baking sheet and chill for at least 20 minutes before cutting into the desired shapes.

To cook the puff pastry, place the cut pieces onto a slightly dampened baking sheet (by being damp the puff pastry will stay in place and not slide all over the baking sheet when you go to egg wash it).

Usually puff pieces are egg washed on top, which gives them their lovely golden and shiny appearance when cooked. This also allows you to decorate the top if you wish, by 'drawing', carefully, simple designs onto the egg wash.

Puff pastry needs to be cooked in a hot oven to puff up properly. Put the pieces in at about 200°C/400°F/Gas 6. The temperature can be turned down after the first 10 minutes to about 180°C/350°F/Gas 4 and then the cooking is continued for another 10–15 minutes. This ensures that the puff pieces are cooked right through and the middles won't be a soggy mass of uncooked dough.

savoury shortcrust pastry

Just flour, water and butter can produce a satisfactory result, but we like to enrich this shortcrust with eggs and cream. It can be made either by hand or in a food processor.

Makes about 900 g (2 lb)

500 g (1 lb 2 oz) plain flour
25 g (1 oz) caster sugar
2 teaspoons salt
375 g (13 oz) unsalted butter, chilled and diced
2 eggs
2 tablespoons single cream

You make this pastry either by hand or by pulsing in a food processor. Place all the dry ingredients into a chilled bowl. Add the butter and rub it in until the mixture is pea-size consistency.

Mix together the eggs and cream. Pour into the bowl and mix until it all comes together.

Transfer to your work surface and, with the heels of your hand, work until the mixture holds together nicely. Wrap well in clingfilm and chill for at least an hour. This firms up the butter and allows the gluten in the flour to relax.

Divide into 3 portions, wrap well and, if not using immediately, store in the fridge for up to 1 week or freezer for up to 1 month.

sweet shortcrust pastry

This shortcrust is crisp yet tender pastry, very workable. The more sugar a shortcrust dough has, the 'shorter' and harder it becomes to work with. The secret is to remember to keep everything cool, both ingredients and the bowl. Chill for 20–30 minutes before rolling and the same again after rolling and lining the tart tin. This will give the best results because the butter will not have the opportunity to melt, which can make the pastry heavy and dense. It's worth making in the quantity below and then freezing what you don't use the first time around.

Makes about 900 g (2 lb)

650 g (1 lb 7 oz) soft flour
175 g (6 oz) caster sugar
350 g (12 oz) unsalted butter, chilled and diced
3 eggs
A pinch of salt

You make this pastry by hand or by pulsing in a food processor. Place the flour and sugar in a chilled bowl. Add the butter and rub it in until the mixture is pea-size consistency. Stir together the eggs, pour into the bowl, add the salt and mix until the mixture comes together.

Transfer the mixture to your work surface and, using the heel of your hand, work the mixture until it all holds together in a cohesive ball and there are no big lumps of butter unmixed. Divide into four even batches, wrap well in clingfilm and chill. This pastry will keep in the fridge for about 1 week and in the freezer for about 1 month.

note on baking blind

Many recipes call for blind baking a tart base. This is simply a pre-baking of the base, which is accomplished by lining the base with greaseproof paper or kitchen foil and filling with dry beans of some sort. This holds the pastry in place until it has cooked enough to be set. The pastry is cooked with this blind bake in place for about 15 minutes at 190°C/375°F/Gas 5. Often, after removing the beans and paper or foil, the tart base is popped back into the oven for a minute or two to ensure that the bottom is evenly cooked to a golden brown.

A useful tip is to brush the base and the sides of the cooked pastry with egg yolk to seal the pastry. This is especially helpful when the filling is a runny type, such as with the Lemon-scented Cheese and Berry Tartlets on page 197 or the Lemon Tart on page 199.

index

Page numbers in *italic* indicate pictures